T0146584

Bits of Life

Bits of Life

Bitsy Bowman

 iUniverse®

BITS OF LIFE

iUniverse books may be ordered through booksellers or by contacting:

iUniverse
1663 Liberty Drive
Bloomington, IN 47403
www.iuniverse.com

1-800-Authors (1-800-288-4677)

Because of the dynamic nature of the Internet, any web addresses or links contained in this book may have changed since publication and may no longer be valid. The views expressed in this work are solely those of the author and do not necessarily reflect the views of the publisher, and the publisher hereby disclaims any responsibility for them.

Any people depicted in stock imagery provided by Thinkstock are models, and such images are being used for illustrative purposes only.

Certain stock imagery © Thinkstock.

ISBN: 978-1-5320-3774-0 (sc)
ISBN: 978-1-5320-3775-7 (e)

Library of Congress Control Number: 2017918257

Print information available on the last page.

iUniverse rev. date: 02/08/2018

Contents

Dedication

This book is dedicated to the many readers of my newspaper columns, my numerous friends and my loving family. My sincere wish is that all who read these words may experience warmth, joy and perhaps shed just a few tears.

Introduction

One day, while Bitsy and I were living in Wichita, Kansas, I came home for lunch to find a round, black, charred spot on the kitchen floor. Of course, I knew what had happened. Bitsy was a smoker then and she had emptied a hot ash tray into the kitchen waste basket, caught it on fire and burned the floor but being a considerate husband I gave her an opportunity to explain by asking "What happened?" She calmly stated "Would you believe <u>spontaneous combustion</u>?" I replied, "You don't even know what that means." She replied, "Well, I know it's not my fault!" To be both quick witted and funny are great traits to have especially when your vocation is writing.

Her syndicated newspaper columns (written under her nickname "Bitsy") are filled with humor, reality, some sadness and much love. Her columns, under the title "Bits of Life," very well defines their content. I have selected several of her columns and put them into this book format which has also been titled "Bits of Life." Each column stands alone and is unrelated to any other column except that Bitsy's writing talent fills each one. The Table of Content will guide you to each subject.

This book of her columns will bring back memories to you, fill you with much laughter and perhaps a few tears, but most of all you will be entertained.

Sam S. Bowman

A Camper I'm Not

My family was discussing vacation plans the other day. Someone suggested camping out. My husband laughed and said, "Your mother's idea of roughing it is staying at a plushy motel with room service." I accepted the challenge and reminded him of the time we camped out years ago. "Some campout," he said. "We stayed all of five hours." The boys became interested and wanted to hear the entire story.

We were to meet some friends a few miles from our home at a lake with campsites nearby. (I never understood why people drag all that camping equipment to drive down the road and set it up all again.)

Knowing that I wouldn't last too long, my husband packed very few camping items in the car although I insisted that we take enough for the weekend.

We met our friends, visited and enjoyed a swim in the lake. After dinner it was getting very hot and the mosquitoes were eating me up. I helped with the dishes out of a tin pan which didn't look too sanitary to me. There was so much to put up. Everything had to be packed back into its place. It looked to me like one of those puzzles with 850 pieces: one wrong move and the puzzle wouldn't fit together.

Some child came by proudly dangling a dead snake which he had just caught. I felt sick. My husband grinned and asked, "How about setting up our sleeping gear?" "Are you kidding?" I said. "It's hot, the mosquitoes are holding a convention on my legs, snakes are running wild all over the place. I'd be safer sleeping on a busy train track."

1

"Had enough?" he said. "Don't rub it in," I answered. "With 35 insect bites, I'm just not feeling too well tonight." We went home.

The boys loved that story. It confirmed their belief that I was a hot house plant. They could go camping on their own. I'll stay home and try to find someone to talk to. There must be a few people like me in the world. Surely everyone doesn't want to spend their vacation with snakes and mosquitoes.

A Christmas Lesson Well Learned

This is an after Christmas story of sacrifice, love and growing up. On Christmas morning my children were more excited about my opening their gift to me than they were about their own gifts.

They handed me a package which said "To mom from all your boys." Inside was a note telling me to look for a package under the tree which had no name tag on it. When I found that one, there was another note inside directing me to another box. In that box was a note instructing me to look for the tiny box at the bottom of the larger one to find a "treasure."

Inside the tiny box was a treasure indeed - a beautiful ivory and gold elephant pendant. I had seen it months before and admired it.

As the story unraveled, I learned that my middle son had gone to the jewelry store and explained it to the owner that he and his brothers wanted to give me the elephant for Christmas. She (the owner) kindly reduced the elephant to within their financial reach. My son asked her to hold the elephant until he could get the money together and then mail it.

After months of leaf raking, saving and denying himself a pair of Western boots my son had a large share to pay on the gift. His brothers chipped in by giving money which was sent mostly to them for Christmas. They had taken their own gifts and used it to buy one for me. Then their Dad helped with the arrangements and the elephant was ordered, delivered and hidden until Christmas morning.

Then, this same son decided that he wanted to give gifts which would fill a Christmas stocking like the one he always got. Since he had no stockings, he used drawers in the chest which we use for toys. The boys removed the toys and wrote name cards for each drawer: "Mom, Dad, Aunt Punk, Grandmother and Granddaddy."

Each drawer contained a long strip of candy canes, mints, gum and small, personal gifts for each individual person. The chest was then sealed and taped closed with a note warning us not open until Christmas morning.

Happy faces and excited eyes watched us open the drawers and find our gifts just as they watched me search for and find a box with a wonderful elephant.

My children had discovered the gift of giving. They learned that it was truly more joyful to give than to receive because they had sacrificed, worked and planned to give gifts that brought great pleasure to the recipients.

They were growing up. It is sad but also it is beautiful. The beauty is knowing that to possess a generous heart is truly a blessing.

A Different Christmas

Christmas this year was an experience not like others in the past. We have a house full of grown and almost grown children and the excitement of years gone by did not linger long.

Christmas morning started like all the others except that we forgot to get movie film to capture for later years the fun of watching the boys as they opened their gifts. (Now that I think of it, I have not seen the movies of the past three holidays but I suppose they are recorded for posterity.}

Everyone enjoyed passing around gifts from under a beautiful tree which had become so dry that pine needles fell off in masses. By the time we were finished, the tree held few needles - just sticks and branches which made strange shapes like something from the "ET" movie.

As the boys carried their gifts upstairs, each in turn informed us that they had plans for the afternoon. One was going deer hunting and asked that Christmas dinner be ready early - two hours earlier than we had planned. Another son had a date and the youngest son said he was going to ride his new, small motorcycle all day and thank you very much.

My astonished husband looked me and asked, "What is wrong with these kids? They used to stay home all day and enjoy their gifts." Sadly I answered that they were growing up and immediately felt 10 years older myself. The day passed with young people coming in and out (mostly out) and the phone ringing all afternoon with calls from their friends who were trying to locate them.

This must be some turning point in our lives which we should accept with grace. That's what I keep telling myself as I watched them go out the door. The days of the past are gone when the boys played with toys and childish laughter filled the house.

Yet we must accept our blessings where we find them and being together as a family on that day - if even for a brief time - should be a time to remember and to cherish. Someday they all may be unable to spend Christmas with us.

As I write this, I see two pictures on my desk of two little boys on Santa's lap. They were 3 and 5 years old at the time. Today they are 14 and 16.

My husband keeps lamenting that our family has lost the spirit of Christmas but what he is really saying is: "Where have all the children gone?"

May your New Year be filled with happiness and may you recognize and be thankful for your blessings wherever you find them.

A Neat Freak I'm Not

Some women always look so neat and well turned out. No matter what they wear, they always look stylish and attractive. Then there are people like me who appear as if they have just rushed out of the laundromat and are wearing the clothes they just washed.

It is very frustrating to be in that last category. No matter how hard I try, I have a last-minute disaster and go out looking like the sinking Titanic.

One Easter many years ago, I proudly wore my new black suit and hat to church. I felt great that morning because I thought I looked well-dressed. When I came home and was hanging up the suit, there on the clothes rack was the skirt to my new black suit. (To this day I don't know how that happened.) I looked down at the skirt I had worn and discovered that it was an old black one that didn't match the top - quite.

I recently went to a football game out of town and was told to dress for rain. I walked into the stadium wearing tennis shoes, my clear, plastic drizzle boots over them, a rain hat that looked like a large plastic flower with wilted pedals and there wasn't a drop of rain all night. See what I mean?

The same is true with my voice and image. I always wanted a deep, husky voice like Lauren Bacall. Instead I got the type of voice that causes people to ask when I answer the phone, "Is your mother at home?" or "Dear, may I speak to the lady of the house?"

When I was a little girl I wanted to grow up to be a mysterious lady. I wanted to be sleek and complicated and have people say, "You never know what she's thinking, she's so mysterious and exotic." Instead people see me as a rushed, confused, disheveled woman who is always driving carpools and has three notes hanging in the car and two stuck to my purse with tape. That definitely is not a mysterious image!

I was discussing this problem with a friend and she agreed that some women just naturally have style and class. I mentioned one woman whom I thought was just perfect looking and had all the physical qualities I would like to have.

My friend said, "I agree, she is ravishing but didn't you know that she spends a fortune taking yearly trips to an exclusive reducing salon? She's also had a 'nose job' and surgery to have her stomach 'tucked'." I could hardly believe it, but it made my day. I always thought she was born that beautiful.

Absentmindedness

What in the world do you do with children who constantly lose things? Until recently, I have had that problem with only one of my three children. I figured that one out of three isn't bad.

However my youngest son, who has gone to a different school this year, has just suddenly been stricken with total absentmindedness. In one week, he lost two lunch tickets and a library book. He first said he gave me the book and lunch tickets and that I lost them. When he found out I wasn't going to take the rap for him, he suddenly, "remembered" he left all the items at his friend's house. I've called his friend so many times about this that I expect their friendship to end and that his family will report me to the telephone company for harassment.

This was once my organized child. He always knew where his things were and never forgot his homework. I have about come to the conclusion that when children enter junior high school a transformation comes over them. They change in many ways, but the first thing to go is their memory. I've heard that they "grow up" then and maybe that's true. If forgetfulness is a sign of growing up, then this child has reached that stage in a few weeks that he's been in school.

It is strange that he remembers the name, phone numbers and addresses of his friends. Also, he remembers the location of the refrigerator, soda pop, snacks and the television set. He recalls with perfect clarity that his brother borrowed $1.60 from him two months ago and hasn't repaid him yet.

When he needs money, he remembers to ask. When he has volunteered me to drive him and his friends somewhere, he remembers that. And he certainly recalls every time I have been late getting him at school since he entered the first grade.

Perhaps this is a temporary condition that will pass. But it is certainly embarrassing and time-consuming to have to call all the places we have been the last week asking about that library book. Considering the lunch tickets, I did call the school and asked them to search. If found, I asked them to hang the tickets around his neck or stapled them to him.

The next time he asks for money. I won't remember.

After Vacation Disaster

Summer vacations can be wonderful for renewing your spirit and resting. The shock is returning home. Most people are glad to get home but at that point I could be a gypsy and wander the face of the earth. Perhaps I have this attitude because of what I faced when I came home. It's called "After Vacation Disaster!"

After two weeks of fun and sun (and even a 6 mile canoe trip), I returned home to a sink full of dirty dishes-compliments of my oldest son. While washing dishes, I was also doing a large load of clothes in the washing machine. I didn't notice the younger children changing three times a day but someone wore all those clothes.

While I was washing everything in sight, I was told that the doorknob had fallen off, the dishwasher was making a rattling sound like a tea kettle boiling over. The frostless refrigerator suddenly developed frost and water was running from the top to the vegetable bins in the bottom. The icemaker suddenly refused to make ice. (That icemaker is temperamental and takes a rest often anyway.)

The next day the television set lost its color. Then the exhausted washing machine started making a strange noise which sent me into a nervous frenzy because that washing machine and I are a team.

I almost got the feeling that because I went away the appliances decided to take a vacation also. Perhaps they need constant use to keep them in good working order.

Looking over the situation at home, I am faced with three choices: suffering through all these repairs; selling the house and leaving all the appliances and starting over again. Maybe I can find that bearded man who rents canoes and get myself lost on the river.

Almost Grown Children

A group of friends (all parents) got together recently and the conversation turned to their "almost grown" children who had moved out of the house. Some parents are devastated when this happens and others have the misguided notion that they will, at least, have freedom. The parents whose children moved a great distance away take the situation much harder at first and then they learn to cope with "it". On the other hand, the parents who children move out and remain in the same town offer the most interesting comments.

One father reported that he had not found a decent tie in his closet since his son "borrowed a few ties" the day he left home. Another said, "Yeah, well you think that is a problem. My son calls on the same day every month and hints broadly that he is a little short on rent money and suggests sinister actions which will be taken against him if we don't chip in and help out. We discussed this apartment before he left and he said he could handle it financially."

A mother spoke up and laughingly remarked that she thought her laundry chores would be reduced when her daughter moved out. But now she finds that her daughter brings a two week washing home to "do later" and the clothes sit there for days until her mother washes them. When the daughter returns, she always says the same thing, "Oh mother, you **shouldn't** have done that for me. I was going to wash those clothes myself. I just wanted to drop them off while I was out this way." This same kid checks her mother's closet for "new" dresses and asks to try them on and perhaps borrow one or two for special events.

Then an irate couple broke in and said with bitterness, "At least you're dealing with your own kids. We have a roommate problem." All of us looked at them with shocked attention until they explained they were talking about their son's roommate. It seems that the two boys (age 19) decided to share an apartment and all the expenses. They divided up the duties even including who would get the washing powder each week. These kids were really organized. Or so it seemed! Then the roommate had financial troubles resulting from his constant entertainment and you can guess who got stuck with most of the bills. After six months, the roommate failed out of college and left their son with the telephone bill equal to the national debt. It seems that he had friends in foreign countries and he called them all. To make matters worse, he moved from his permanent address and when his son called his former roommate's parents, he found out they were not his parents after all. The roommate has vanished and left no trace.

The last comment comes from a shy lady who said her problem was minor in view of the missing roommate. But she lamented that her daughter told everyone how much she was enjoying her freedom and being "on her own."

"Own her own my foot," the woman remarked, warming to her subject. "She thinks she's on her own." Several times a week she breezes in the house and raids the pantry of canned goods, the freezer of meat, borrows linens and clothes, drops her dirty laundry in the floor, smiles and kisses me goodbye.

When she runs out of food or clothes, whichever comes first, she reappears to repeat the performance. And when asked by a neighbor how she likes living away from home, she had the nerve to say, "I love it. I feel so independent and self-sufficient. And I don't have any trouble with money because I am a good manager. I'm doing great on my grocery bills. It doesn't take all that much to live alone."

America – Still the Best Place to Live

Monday, July 4, is America's birthday. We have come a long ways since a group of people came to this land and decided to form a nation. In recent years, we've been called everything from "Yankees" to "Ugly Americans" but as a people, we still have our national pride.

We are fighting inflation and struggling to survive but we have a right to voice our dissent.

We have a large unemployment rate and are wrestling with social reforms but we still have a thing called elections and a priceless gift call the vote.

We haven't found a complete cure for cancer but doctors and scientists are making headway and we have put a man on the moon.

Some of our politicians may be corrupt but we have a system which eventually brings them to justice and exposes them to the public.

We have both good and bad journalism and good and biased newspapers but we have a free press and people can choose what they wish to read and decide for themselves what they believe.

We are heavily and sometimes unjustly taxed but we are not thrown in prison for complaining or for honestly questioning the government's decisions.

We find dirty books, movies and television shows all around us but we have the right to refuse to read and watch them. Also, we have organizations which try to shield our young children from reading and viewing trash.

Postal rates increase but we can count on the mail arriving six days a week.

Rates for heating and cooling our homes are soaring but most of us are reasonably warm in winter and cool in summer. Admittedly, this is a serious problem when fuel bills approach the cost (and sometimes exceed) the monthly house payment. But in some countries there is no choice because there is no fuel for a vast majority of the people.

We have food on the table while millions are starving elsewhere.

We can vote on politicians without overthrowing the government and executing them.

In times of national stress and tragedy such as the Iranian hostage seizure and the abortive attempt to rescue our people, our country unifies and stands together. Remember the yellow ribbons tied on trees to symbolize our united hope for the return of our citizens.

In our land we have choices and we are free to make them. There is much that is wrong with our country and we live in troubled times yet we are free.

We can write to our state and national leaders and voice our opinions in public without fear of being taken away by a secret police force.

All things considered, there are few of us who would change places with a citizen of another country. And there are citizens of other countries who would be grateful to change places with us.

With all its faults, America's our home and its people-our people. You can feel that emotion when the national anthem is played. And you can feel it when you return from a trip out of the country and see the Statue of Liberty standing tall and proud.

Perhaps we can improve our country and teach our younger ones who follow us to improve it even more. We have to try. In any case, most of us are very proud to be Americans.

"Happy Birthday America!"

An Overloaded Purse

Ladies, how often do you clean out your pocketbook? Do you have trouble changing from one purse to another? Do you have a favorite purse which you carry all season or all year?

If you answered "Seldom" to the first question and "Yes" to the second and third questions, then you have a problem similar to mine-an overloaded purse.

A woman's favorite purse is rather like a good, familiar mattress-you're used to it, feel comfortable with it and recognize it immediately.

I have been teased often about my large purses but I wouldn't trade them for the world. I really admired the trim, neat, dainty pocketbooks that some ladies use but I can't imagine how they get all their necessities inside.

I tried a small, elegant purse once and it was a disaster. I had to carry half of my items in my coat and the other half in my husband's coat and pockets. Yes, he did object strongly! All evening I was searching my pretty mini-purse, my coat, his coat and his pockets and it wasn't worth the hassle.

He always told me that someday my purse would explode from overload and on a street in St. Louis, the seams in my purse literally gave way and expired leaving the contents everywhere. He had his revenge that day.

No matter what he says I decided long ago that I had to be myself (messy and keep those huge pocketbooks.) I think he and I have a different definition of "necessities." He has listed half the items in my purse is nonessential. However, I consider the following items for everyday and emergency use: Kleenex, handkerchiefs, prescription reading glasses, sunglasses, matches, notes like the laundry and grocery lists, cards from shops I have visited, wallet, pictures, brush and comb, toothbrush and toothpaste, nail file, hairpins, aspirin, and high priority notes like "today's errands and lists for dinner tonight", cosmetic case, smelling salts, Band-Aids, scissors, stationary (in case I have a minute to write a letter), a paperback book (in case I have another minute to read), diet sweetener and occasionally a tiny package of mustard and catchup (one never knows.)

If you carry one half of these items, we are kindred spirits and should hope that the old Art Linklater television program is revived. Remember when Art selected a lady from the audience and named an unusual item? If she had it in her purse, she won a prize.

I'll bet that seven out of ten of you ladies have some of those items in your purse today. If you do, call me and together we will contact Art Linklater.

An Unusual Way for Scoring At Bridge

Some of my friends have come up with an unusual idea for scoring at bridge. This method can only be used among friends as no one else will ever understand it.

We thought it up when we realized that some of us have been playing casual bridge for over 20 years and cannot keep score yet. (One lady's husband asked her suspiciously where she had been going all those years when she said she was playing bridge.)

The intelligent few who know how to keep score often score differently and we found ourselves scoring one way at one table and another way and a second table. Since we talk and laughed more than we play cards, we decided to score on different things other than card points.

Scoring rules for people who don't play serious bridge:

1. If you arrive on time, add 100 points.
2. If you have fingernail polish on, deduct 50 points. If the polish is cracked, add 25 points.
3. If you wore stockings on bridge day, deduct 75 points unless the stockings have a run. In that case, you get 75 points for the run in the hose (each foot.) White socks add 100 points to your score.
4. If you have a good week and no complaints for us to talk about, deduct 100 points.
5. If the home of the hostess is spotless, which gives the rest of us a complex, the hostess loses 200 points.
6. If you are serious about your cards and get upset with a bad hand, deduct 100 points.
7. If, however, you adapt a "devil may care" attitude and bid widely and double emotionally, add 150 points to your score for being "gutsy."

8. If the hostess serves wine at lunch, she automatically gets 250 points and will be asked to have the group again soon.

9. If any member has just been to the beauty parlor, deduct 75 points; however, for those of us who look like we need to go to the beauty parlor, we get the 75 points added to our score.

10. If any member has gone one month (since the last meeting) without having a sick child at home, or having a child anywhere who did not ask for money, she has to deduct the big 300 points. Her life is going much too smoothly and the rest of us are envious.

As A Teenage Love Advisor, I Resign

The time has come for me to withdraw from the advisor capacity to teenagers in love. Being an advisor and confident is frustrating, expensive and somewhat futile. I found that out the hard way.

My cousin's son decided that he loved being in love. It seemed easier to talk to me than his parents so he started asking my advice. Since my own sons never asked my advice, I was flattered that someone did. (We all know that others cannot resist giving advice.)

"I love Jeannie, Marianne and Vicki in that order." Each time he declared this, he said he was desperately in love with each of them - in that order.

My mistake was to stake him financially. I ordered a rosebud for Jeannie, carnations for Marianne and a gardenia for Vicki. The romances moved along with Marianne and we were on the verge of sending her a dozen roses when they broke up. (Thank goodness I found out before I placed the order.) He was devastated!

It upset me to pay for a rosebud and vase for Jeannie who has already found someone else. Also, Marianne, after their breakup, transferred to another school taking her carnations with her.

I staked my hopes on Vicki and went so far as to invest in a Valentine card that was as large as my shower door. (His idea.) Then Vicki and my cousin's son had an argument and he declared that it was "over forever." I was sympathetic but wondered what we would do with that huge Valentine card. That problem didn't seem to bother him but he didn't pay six dollars for the card. I did.

Now, he has his eye on another girl who is "beautiful and cool." I have been trying to explain why I haven't helped him all that much and that maybe he should appoint his own mother as his advisor. He should realize that I am not very capable since I showed such bad judgment as to purchase a Valentine card in January. I should have waited until February 12.

I can only hope that his new love is "beautiful and cool," will not like flowers nor candy but will enjoy receiving a huge, gigantic Valentine card which has been in my closet for over a month. I guess there is always hope!

Aunt Punk Has the Patience of Job

My 70-year-old aunt is the bravest person I know. After spending several months with us and enduring a life style with two teenagers in the house, she decided to take our youngest son back to Tennessee with her for a visit. (She was already on the verge of collapse when she left to return home.)

She arrived home to find our oldest son living in her house while he worked the summer in Nashville. He had renovated the house to make himself comfortable. He also had a new puppy, a bulldog named Sampson, who was not housebroken. (I'm such a coward that I am glad I was not there to see her expression when she arrived.)

Just as she was unpacking, she learned that the older son had two jobs and would not be there the evening except for meals, of course. That meant that Sampson was in her charge. The youngest son vowed that he would care for the dog but you can imagine how long that "newness" lasted. Then within a week of her return, Sampson had to have an emergency eye surgery. (I know who paid the bill without even asking.)

Our house, for the first time in many years, has been supremely quiet. We had the nerve to tell her that over a long distance phone call and she threatened to hang up the phone. I was told how her furniture had been rearranged, how the dog still did not respond to training, how she hired a neighbor to build a doghouse, how the dog cried at 5 AM every morning, how the youngest son told her he was bored and slept most of the day, how both boys wanted to put cable-television in her house and on and on.

We have been afraid to call her again. We fear that she may have thrown both boys and the dog out in the street or entered herself into a hospital. This is a clear case of not realizing the danger and hazards on the job before you undertake it.

So I sat in blissful solitude writing this column and in the back of my mind I listened for the phone. I expect a collect call from the bus station telling me to come and get two boys and a bulldog.

I really wouldn't blame her for evicting them all. After all, why should I enjoy all the peace and quiet?

Aunt Punk to the Rescue

Dealing with stress and tension is a difficult problem for many of us today. Recently after six weeks full of activities, unusual stressful events (like a car wreck) and the everyday routine of chores, errands, carpools and all the many things a housewife does for her family, I suddenly declared myself a "basket case."

My family decided it was time to call in the reserves. The reserves in our family is my aunt who is 74 years young and has more pep and energy than I ever had on the best day of my life. She informed me that she would take charge for several days while I rested and she remarked that I should "calm down" and handle my stress with more courage and faith. Capable though she is, I thought, "Oh yeah, just wait!"

I gave her a list of chores for the first day. She started out with vigor. She went to the cleaners, the bank, the insurance company and the grocery. When she checked in for lunch, it was time for her to get one of the boys at school and take him for an allergy shot.

By 3 p.m. she was "lagging" a little but would not admit it. Then it was time to get one of the boys at wrestling practice. After that pick-up it was time to get another boy at basketball practice. At 6 p.m. she dragged herself in and mentioned that we had to think about cooking dinner.

By 8 p.m., she was looking for her bed, her robe and her medicine. I heard her tell one of the boys that she could not find her house slippers and without them she would surely catch "atheltic's foot" walking around our house with so many boys living here. We asked her if she meant athlete's foot and she answered, "Yes, I get it every time I come here."

Then I heard her scrambling around in her luggage. She was looking for her aspirins, arthritis medicine and anything else that may ease her pain. Her feet had collapsed and the rest of her was sinking fast.

I couldn't resist asking her how she was dealing with her stress. She looked up at me and said, "How can you take all this confusion, constant running around and no definite schedule for meals because everyone comes home in shifts?"

Smiling to myself, I thought of an old Indian proverb: "Never judge a person until you have walked in his moccasins for a week."

Behavior on the Elevator

My husband recently remarked about the strange and consistent behavior of people on an elevator. Have you noticed that they never talk to strangers, invariably look at the number buttons on the wall or stare at the lighted numbers designating the floors as the elevator moves from one floor to another?

When recently we are on a trip, my husband swears that I did just that every time we stepped on the elevator. He won't believe me when I tell him that I was praying to get to our destination— on the 24th floor of the hotel. I panicked every time we took that elevator. It was a half-glass affair where you could gaze out and see the town. But I saw the movie, "The Towering Inferno," and remembered what happens to all those people who were trying to escape on that glass elevator.

Also, I had read the signs on each floor: "In case of fire, do not use the elevator." That didn't comfort me on the 24th floor. I could not imagine even the Bionic Man running down 24 flights of stairs and still having some hope of getting out safely in case of fire.

My husband mentioned that every time we got on the elevator it was full of passengers. With all those different people from all walks of life, no one spoke as we passed from floor to floor except to say what floor they wanted and they all stared at the lighted numbers as be passed from floor to floor.

I had never really considered the silence on elevators before. Perhaps each elevator in large hotels should have a hostess (since elevator operators are rarely used now) to start a conversation. People could wear name tags with their home or business address. If you saw someone from your state or hometown that would break the ice and you can chat.

My husband's best idea was to say something outrageous to get the passengers attention and start a conversation. He thought of various things and came up with some openers: "Pardon me, madam, but your pantyhose have fallen down." "Sir, excuse me but I thought you would want to know that your trousers are ripped in the seat." "Now that we are assembled here on this elevator, everyone smile as Candid Camera is observing us. Look natural and don't stare at the wall or the floor."

Personally, since elevator trips are brief, I don't think his idea will work. Rather, I think if we had attempted those remarks, we would have been arrested or taken away by men in white coats with a butterfly net. But it would have been an interesting experiment to try.

Being Thankful on Thanksgiving

On Thanksgiving Day, it is time again to give thanks for our blessings and for families to gather together in fellowship and love. This year, I decided to give thanks for the little things in life which we take for granted.

I thank the Lord for my family and for their love for me. That is not a little thing but one too important to be left out. Next, I am thankful for friends who bring so much joy to our lives.

I am thankful for our new minister and his family who, in such a short time, is uniting our church and guides us with love and sensitivity letting us all know that each of us is worthy in his eyes and in the eyes of God.

I am grateful for the smile of strangers, the helping hand given when it was most needed like a young Manchester, Tennessee couple who helped me when I had car trouble on an interstate 100 miles from Nashville.

I am thankful when my family overlooks why sharp words, my anger and crossness on bad days, yet they continued to love me and realize that, I too, am human and may be tired.

I am thankful for a husband and children who understand me and care for me in spite of my faults. And for parents and aunts and uncles whose faces brightened when I see them and who never forget me.

I thank the Lord that my sons have minds to reason, to think, to feel, to be interested in the world around them.

I am thankful for the fragile peace which we enjoy and pray that it may continue always.

I thank the Lord for people who have faced great hardships and sadness yet they inspire me and others with their courage and their faith.

I am thankful for dedicated doctors and nurses who seek to heal us. And for the teachers who set good examples in our schools when our children are groping with the problems of growing up. And for all the people in our schools who provide a service in some way to our children which touches their lives.

I am thankful for each day and the fact that I'm here to face it. Often we don't appreciate the fact that we are blessed to be able to awaken to a new day full of challenges and stand on our feet to meet those challenges.

As I reviewed those things which make me feel thankful: love, family, friendship, a new minister, his family and the church, peace, the helping hand of strangers, intelligence, dedicated doctors and nurses, inspiration, schools and teachers and life itself, I realize that those things are not little at all. They are the basic foundation of our being, yet I don't always appreciate them. Too often, I take all this for granted but on Thanksgiving Day, I realize how important all these people and factors are and I feel blessed again.

Happy Thanksgiving and many blessings to you and your loved ones.

Birthdays Are For Men

Many of my "young" friends are having 40th birthdays. That must be the most painful year to overcome-especially for women.

Some have asked my advice. I tried telling them that I'd let them know when I got there but they just laughed and said, "Who are you trying to kid?" So I'll tell the truth.

The first thing to do is to approach that year with a good mental attitude. Think things like: "I'm glad I made it this far" and "I'm like a fine old wine I become rarer with age." Tell your friends that those little lines at the corners of your eyes are laugh lines. They mean that you have experienced life to the fullest. Never call those lines "crow's feet."

Then check your health. Let's face it, it isn't as great as it was at 20. Just try to think 20 and take care of your 40 year old body. I will give you some snappy answers to some medical problems that affect some 40-plus people.

Nervousness: "I'm just high strung from having led such an exciting life."

Bifocals: "I didn't really need those but I didn't want to miss anything (like reading the newspaper.)

Orthopedic shoes: "Take up golf, hiking or birdwatching and swear those shoes were recommended for that sport."

Personally, I think being 40 is the pits but the secret is to smile and pretend you don't care.

A neighbor once asked me, "How do you feel about being 40?" I lied and said, "It's great, life begins at 40 doesn't it?" Then she really stopped me! She asked, "How do you know when you are going through the change of life?"

I smiled and said, "When you are constantly looking out your window and waiting for a Hollywood movie star to ride up on his motorcycle and take you away.

Black Monday

"Black Monday" has come at our house. It was the first day of football practice. It's the same every year.

First, we hope for cool weather. If that fails, we wish for summer rain. We send our sons off and pray for them as they leave the house.

Football insurance is paid up. Their teeth are counted and accounted for. The practice shoes ($85 each) are killing their feet. (The shoes are not paid for yet.) Their father reminds them that they should have run 3 miles every day since school was out. At this point, they should be doing 100 push-ups a day minimum. Personally, if I had to train like that, I'd either be buried by now or be the Bionic Woman.

All day we wait for their return. Everyone in the family wants to be the first one to spot them and report the damage.

Comments run like this: "Wonder how they are doing?" "Wonder who has passed out yet?" "What's the temperature outside?" I've noticed that the younger children have the most gruesome remarks.

Today, I heard. "Hey mom, guess why the cemetery is so close to the football field?" Answer: "The coaches won't have to walk so far to throw the dead bodies." Great laughter follows that remark as I reach for an aspirin and check the phone numbers of the family doctor, bone specialist, orthodontist and plastic surgeon.

A light rain starts to fall. I rejoice until it turns to thunder and lightning. Then little brother strolls in to cheer me up. "Don't worry mom, they won't practice close to the trees. The coaches always take them right out in the middle of the field to play when it's lightning." (This kid will certainly be an undertaker. He's absolutely enjoying himself.)

By 6:30 PM I am seriously considering driving by the cemetery, then we hear the car turning into the driveway. The fallen heroes return looking like each step may be their last and they would welcome it.

A cleat is broken off from the new shoes, their feet are covered with blisters, arms are bruised, faces are flushed; their hair and clothes are so wet and dirty that I consider throwing the boys-with clothes on-into the washer.

They mumble: "Gimme me some water, not hungry, where's the ice packs?" It's started again. From now until the last game of the season, the house will smell of liniment for aching muscles.

There will be no more ice except for ice packs. The hot water will be restricted for medical purposes-hot water bottles and soap baths. My car will carry a cheering family to all the scrimmages and games. It will go on and on and on.

This, dear friends, is the great American sport known as football.

Bridge Group Treasures

My bridge group was having lunch at the home of a member. The delicious dessert started a conversation about kitchen appliances and utensils. The hostess told us that she had used a spring-form pan to make the cheesecake. A few of us didn't know what a spring-form pan was. (I thought it sounded like a mini-trampoline for the "Barbie" doll.) But most of the group not only knew about the pan but wanted one.

Then a friend looked at me and asked, "Did you ever get your cover for that large Silverstone skillet?" Another lady said she didn't have the cover either. Someone asked her, "You mean you have a Silverstone skillet too?" She laughed and answered, "Well, you don't think I would let Bitsy and Mary have a Silverstone skillet without buying one for myself, do you?"

Suddenly, all laughed and realized that things we had in our kitchens were being discussed like status symbols.

One lady said, "I have the "Fry Daddy.' Does anyone else have that?" Only one other person did. One sad voice asked, "I have the 'Fry Baby.' "Does that count?"

Mary reasserted her position by saying, "I'm still the only one with a cover for my Silverstone skillet." "Don't be such a snob," we all said. Another woman mentioned that she was just lusting for a "Dust Buster." (That sounded like a disguised secret agent to me.) The "Dust Buster" I learned, is used to remove dust from steps and cars and hard-to-reach places where a vacuum is too large or awkward to reach.

I mentioned my vegetable steamer thinking I was the only one there who had one. Mary said, "Remember, I recommended that to you? I've had one for ages."

I tried again with a food processor, a plastic flower that opens jars, a glass lid that keeps a pan of water from boiling over and corn-on-the-cob holders. My last shot was an unusual spoon which makes butter patties look like little shells. I was out voted by the lady who had a pair of tiny wooden tongs to remove toast from the toaster.

After the luncheon, I left thinking how inadequate my kitchen was stocked. Thinking I may investigate the spring-form pan, I went to the shopping center where I saw half of the bridge club looking for that pan, the Silverstone skillet, the Dust Buster and other items mentioned that day.

It takes so little to make us housewives happy and so many gadgets to achieve status in the kitchen.

Car Trip Memories

I was looking through some old photographs recently. My eyes filled with tears when I saw pictures of the children and realized how very small they were just a few years ago. But when my husband saw my sad expression, I told him how I long for the "good old days" when the boys were little again.

"Remember the time when we started on a five hour trip and I forgot to pack the diapers?" I laughed. "I will never forget that." He said grimly. "The baby had one diaper on and one spare. You spent the entire time drying out the wet one in the wind outside the rolled up window. Everyone on the highway thought it was an emergency signal," he said.

"Well, what about the fun we had taking the baby to his first drive-in movie?" "What fun?" He grumbled. "I waited in the car for 30 minutes while you packed the entire house: baby bottles, toys, blankets, diaper bag, pillows, car seat and portable bed. We could have taken a trip with all that junk and we were only going to a movie."

"I also remember that we set through that terrible first feature waiting to see the good second one. Ten minutes after it started, the baby started screaming his head off. Car horns started blowing. I left so fast that I tore the speaker off the post and didn't even know it. We were lucky we didn't get arrested."

He didn't seem to be enjoying the trip down memory lane. I decided to try a different approach.

"Well, didn't we have a lot of unusual babysitters?" I asked. "We sure did," he answered. "One lady charged according to the behavior of the children. Do you remember that I paid that woman $50 for two hours and the house was a total wreck?"

"Do you also remember the one who would never let us know she was coming until the last minute?" He asked. "She always said, 'I can sit if nothing happens.' I'm sure she was praying for a flood or a tornado."

He certainly does have negative memories of the good old days. I guess he has lost his is sense of humor.

Children Love Summer Vacation, I Think

Do you know any child who doesn't look forward to summer vacation? They can hardly wait for the end of school. In April, spring fever sets in. As the days get warmer, the children become more restless and less able to concentrate. By May, they are in a frenzy to head for the great outdoors, freedom from school, the swimming pools and lakes, fishing trips and all those fun things that mean summer vacation.

After school is out, they sleep the first week and you have to search for them to announce meals. Then what happens the second week school is out? You guessed it! They are bored, restless and their routine is gone. Conversations go like this: "I'm bored. What's there to do? Boy, is this a vacation? None of my friends are home. I've called six people and they all are gone. I guess they are taking an exciting trip." Yes, the grass is greener down the street at all their friend's houses.)

We steered our children to summer jobs of mowing lawns with hints that they can become tycoons in three short months. The brothers formed a partnership which lasted about 45 minutes. They are still working at their "business" but the partners are not speaking to each other.

Some people send their children off to camp. But I really doubt if any camp would take both of our boys together. How can I ask or expect the counselors to live with all that hostility when I can't bear it myself? We would probably be sued if we sent them together.

However, if one went and the other stayed home, guess what I hear every day? "I sure do miss that brother of mine. He's rotten but

I miss him. Now I don't have anyone to talk to." I add, "You mean that now you don't have anyone not to talk to." (They haven't decoded that remark yet.)

Try a picnic. Ours was great until the boys started a water gun fight and it went too far. I even put them together on a two-mile nature hike. Would you believe they found their way back to the car in record time-and just when I started to drive off after leaving instructions with a ranger that I'd be back in a few days.

Now they want to rent a van and take a long trip. Anyone who travels a long distance with that pair either has a mental problem or will have before they return. After all these years, they must really think I'm stupid to get hooked into a deal like that.

They don't know it yet but I'm going on a trip. I'm leaving a note: "Bye boys, I'm bored and restless too. Enjoy your summer not speaking to each other and be tycoons when I return. You can write me in care of general delivery but I don't know what city and state I'll be in. Will let you know by late July." (Maybe then, they will realize I'm a lot smarter than they thought.)

Children Never Lose Anything

Why is it that children can never find anything for themselves? It is especially worse in the winter when the weather is so cold that more clothes are required to stay warm.

Take for instance, insulated underwear (if you can find it, that is). I have purchased numerous sets the last few years but they somehow disappear the day before someone wants a pair. The same is true with gloves and stocking caps. Now you see them; now you don't.

Since winter set in, my children have made more trips through clothes than my ancestors did when they crossed the country in covered wagons going west.

And guess who is called each time something is missing? Right—mother. "Hey, Mom, I can't find my gloves **anywhere**. I have searched **all over** the **house**."

My answers are standard like a record repeating itself all day. "Have you looked in your drawer where I always put your gloves?" "When did you have them on last?" "Check your brother's room." That usually brings the same answer of, "Mom, you know he won't let me come into his room."

I think all this is one of the hazards of winter. Housebound family members tend to aggravate each other.

Since Mom is a neutral party, I am the only one allowed in the cluttered domains which my boys called their rooms. Except, of course, for my husband who wouldn't put up with all that temperament and bickering for a minute. His answer (which, by the way, works better than mine) is, "Find your own clothes or stay inside." (He also doesn't spend 14 waking hours trapped inside the house with them during a heavy snow. If he did, he wouldn't be so casual about helping them to find items which will speed their departure into the snow.)

Once I started a "lost and found" box. Everyone liked the idea and contributed stray socks, gloves, caps and other items. However, that wasn't successful because we came up with 12 socks —one of a kind, some hats whose ownership were violently disputed and gloves that just stayed in the box for want of a missing and matching partner.

There is no solution to this problem short of gluing or sewing the clothes on the kids and attaching a sign to each garment which says, "Put me back in the right place and I'll be there when you want me again." Can't you just see children wearing clothes with all those signs!

There must be an answer but I can't find it yet. At this point, my only alternative is to run away for the winter. The drawback to that idea is that I can't find one of my gloves and my headscarf is missing.

Do you think this problem could be contagious?

Children Say It Differently

Often we hear amusing childhood remarks which are worth sharing. And many times the conversation of children is more clear and natural than that of adults. I'm sure that you readers can provide many others and I would welcome the opportunity to hear them. (Send them to me in care of this newspaper.)

One of my sons used to refer to homemade rolls as "hand-made rolls." Another called crossword puzzles, "cross-eyed puzzles." A little friend named Jamie, age 15 months, calls his tennis shoes his "Joe's."

A little fellow named Wayne watched as his mother set a mousetrap with gourmet cheese which she had purchased for the occasion. Both mother and child were tense and were apprehensive as they waited for the trap to spring. Finally, they heard the snap of the trap and both rushed into the closet to find the captured mouse. They spent a great deal of time trying to decide if the mouse was dead. It was. Then the mother, Andrea, had to summon great courage to remove the dead mouse (Her husband was out of town so she couldn't wait for his return and Wayne did not volunteer for the job.) Andrea put on long gloves and a mask and finally used pliers to remove the mouse. (Wayne was watching all this procedure in silence.) Feeling triumphant and proud of herself, she remarked to Wayne that she had more courage than she thought. He looked pensive and then he put his hands on his little hips and said, "Well, what about me? I looked at the mouse."

Corey, age 7, watched intently as his older sister was baptized. He was serious and filled with awe and he noticed all the attention his sister was receiving from the members of the church. He pondered the situation all evening and the next morning he made an announcement to his mother, Connie. His comment was, "I have decided that I want to be advertised too."

42

A youngster in the neighborhood decided to visit his friend next door while his parents were away from the house. When they returned, there was a large note telling them where he was. Then he added, "Be careful when you go in the house. The "attack" dogs are inside and the alarm is on." His parents were greatly amused because the attack dogs were small, gentle family pets. When asked why he described the dogs in that way, he explained that he didn't want a burglar to hurt his dogs. (No matter if the family heirlooms were taken but just don't bother the dogs!)

How touching, simple and true are the remarks and intentions of little children and how close they really are to the point at the heart of the matter when they talk. It's a pity that we adults lose this quality because the pressures of life often force us to become complex and devious.

Children's Chores

Have you ever noticed that there are some chores that children are physically incapable of doing? They could throw a ball with the force of King Kong but they cannot replace the top on the milk bottle. They can climb a tree but are unable to put a new roll of toilet tissue in the holder. They comb and brush their hair for ages-not one piece of hair is allowed out of place-yet the ketchup bottle is left with the top off and ketchup running down the side.

They insist on accurate details if they received a phone call and are not home; however, when I miss a call, I am informed 3 months later.

They have the energy to run a 3 mile race but are too weak to carry their dirty clothes to the laundry room. They have plenty of time to ride around town with their friends but just ask them to get you a bottle of milk at the store. In two seconds, you will get four excellent reasons while they are not able to go to the grocery: Big test coming up tomorrow, an English report to write, terrible headache, so exhausted that medical care may be needed.

They can remember the phone numbers of 17 friends but forget to go feed the dog who has lived with us for 15 years. See what I mean?

Next, we come to the manner in which small chores are done-when you are lucky enough to catch a fleeing child.

I asked that all their junk be put out of the way. It was. They moved it all to the next room. When I complained about that, the junk was piled up so high that it looked like the Empire State

Building. They explained that they "put it all in one spot."
(Easier for <u>me</u> to find and put away, I guess.)

No one seems to be responsible for these incidents. We must have
clothes and other items which have a will of their own. Blue
jeans jump out of the dirty clothes basket and attach themselves
to the floor, baseball gloves hide under the sofa, belts are found
lurking under the chairs, baseball shoes decide to live in the
center of the kitchen floor. A baseball bat and a bow and arrow
stayed in the same corner of the family room for one week. I
left them there on purpose-a sort of endurance test. I wanted to
see if anyone would move them. Finally, I called the owners and
demanded that they be moved. They looked up at me with large,
amazed eyes and said, "Gosh, I've been looking for them. I left
them in my room and I don't know how they got here."

The strangest method of helping around the house occurred when
I recently asked my teenager to clean off the kitchen table
after dinner. After he recovered from the shock of my request,
he looked at the table and said "Gross". Then he grabbed his
brothers and told them what "messy eaters" they were. He counted
the crumbs under the table and made them run the vacuum. As
I handed him the sponge, he asked for a hose. "A hose? Do you
mean the garden hose?" I asked in astonishment. "Why do you want
that?" "Well you asked me to clean off the table didn't you?"
He answered.

Christmas Bazaar

One of the nicest things about the Christmas season are the bazaars. Churches, schools and other organizations have them in abundance and they are a treat—especially for women.

There is a trick to attending bazaars. First, you make a list so you won't miss any and arrange them by dates. Then you select the ones that serve food and buy tickets for those first and call it "a night out for the family." That way when your husband and children go along, your dinner is taken care of for the evening. The problem may arise when your husband goes for dinner but doesn't know you are planning a shopping spree also. That's the tricky part.

Some women go early for "baked good" (that sounds innocent enough) and have their husbands and children meet them later for dinner. Others who go as a family have to invent methods of escape in order to shop. I've tried several methods— one is to rush out of the food line when it is still long and we are in the back. I'll say "I'll be back in a minute" and return just as we are next in line to be served. (That method takes perfect timing.) Another is to eat hurriedly and casually remarked, "Everyone finish eating and enjoy your meal while I just dash off for a few seconds and see the craft items."

Unfortunately, my husband has caught on to these methods. At a recent bazaar, I told him that I was looking for lovely, reasonably-priced gift items for Christmas gifts. He eyed me suspiciously but let me leave. When he found me an hour later with the wreath, some cake testers tied with ribbon, two cookbooks and a holiday decoration, he asked if I plan to do <u>all </u>my Christmas shopping there.

The main word to never to use in front of your husband is <u>shopping</u>. That scares a man faster than any other word in the English language. Use words like "browsing, looking, checking prices, searching for bargains" but never "shopping."

Husbands are getting wiser all the time and it's a real challenge to try to stay just half a step ahead of them in the game of shopping at a bazaar.

Christmas Can Be Sweet and Sad

The holiday season is time for remembering. Every Christmas I recall a sweet-sad incident when one of my boys was very young. In every family there seems to be a child who is especially sensitive and caring and a little more attuned to the feelings of others.

I noticed this trait years ago in one of my sons when he was four years old. We had made many trips to the toy shop and every time we visited there, he immediately went over to look at a beautiful, stuffed, fuzzy bear. The large bear was charming and perfect in every detail. I finally decided that the bear would be the perfect choice for him when he awoke on Christmas morning to find it sitting under the tree.

But several weeks before Christmas, he spotted a smaller bear-pale brown with a pinkish tint in his ears. That bear was in a corner behind the other toys and we had not noticed it earlier. When we looked more closely, we noticed that it had only one eye.

My small child was very upset because at his age these lovely animals were like friends to him. We asked the sales lady about the missing eye, thinking that it had fallen off and could be replaced. But she told us that the bear was shipped that way and she was sending it back after Christmas because no one would want it because of the defect.

My son asked me what "defect" meant and I explained. He then asked where the bear would be sent since Santa made all the toys. I casually said, "Oh, I guess he will go back to the North Pole to live."

Tears fell down his cheeks and he said that the poor little bear would never find a home. I tried to cheer him and explained that the bear could live in toy land. "No." He said, "That's like the story of "Rudolph the Red Nosed Reindeer," everyone laughed at Rudolph too." Trying to reassure him I said, "Just look what happened to Rudolph. He became a hero reindeer." But the astute child said, "Rudolph wasn't a hero until he lighted Santa's way with his nose and became important."

"Well, what would make this little bear important?" I asked. He answered simply. "To be loved and wanted over all the other bears and to have a home and not be sent back"

I was astonished. "What about that beautiful bear you like? You have been admiring him for weeks."

He said, "I still like him but I feel sorry for the other one." In his child's logic he explained that the lovely, large bear would never have trouble finding a home but who would want a new bear for Christmas with only one eye? During the last few trips to the store, he checked to see if the "defective" bear was sold and he always came away sad because it was still there.

Of course, I knew then what I had to do. On Christmas morning the little bear with one eye was under the tree with a note from Santa which said, "You are the only person to love and want this little bear so I have brought him to you." That was the happiest child I ever saw and the large, beautiful bear never mentioned.

That was many years ago and the little bear with only one eye still lives with us today.

Christmas Memories

Christmas is coming soon. Children everywhere are counting the days while their fathers are counting the bills and their mothers are counting their blisters on sore and weary feet from shopping.

Our shopping list for toys is definitely 21th century. We search for space creatures and people who inhabit other planets; and dolls that do everything but the dishes and have more friends (for a price, of course) than Will Rogers.

The list is endless and the names for the space characters are so complicated that I sound retarded when I mispronounced them.

What ever happened to the "Betsy - Wetsy" doll and the old brown teddy bear? Now, there's Barbie and Ken and their jet-set friends and Cher and Charlie's Angels. Old Teddy has been replaced by Stretch Armstrong plus Chewbacca and Darth Vader.

But Christmas has another meaning and parents try to impress the serious side not just toys and fun. Every year I am reminded of a sad-funny story with a happy ending which proved to me that perhaps I had instilled a few good values in my children.

Several years ago when the boys were younger, Evil Knievel completely dominated our Christmas preparation. As usual, the boys had asked for everything they saw but the one and only main gift they wanted was a tiny Evil Knievel doll which had just come out in limited supply.

I ordered it in early along with other items. It was my custom to immediately hide all the boxes when they arrived as my boys could sniff out a package miles away. As Christmas drew closer, I sympathized with parents who had not shopped and ordered early and were unable to find the toys they wanted. I secretly congratulated myself for being an early bird. Well, pride goes before the fall!

On Christmas Eve, while my husband was struggling to assemble a toy invented by a mad scientist, I was opening the received packages. There was no Evil Knievel to be found. At first, I didn't believe it. I searched the attic, closets and garage and finally the entire house. Obviously, somewhere in all that mess of papers and boxes was a note telling me that Evil Knievel was not available, but I had never read it in my haste to hide the gifts.

That won't go down as one of my better Christmas Eves. I cried for a long time and considered running away. I even thought about leaving a note saying that Santa needed me to cook for him at the North Pole and I'd be back next year. I simply didn't have the nerve to tell those children that the one toy they wanted most was not there.

I remember that one department store did have two Evils left about a week ago. While I was planning my trip to break in that department store (and working out the consequences of being in jail on Christmas Day), my husband remarked that Christmas wasn't just for receiving gifts and maybe it was time the boys learned that.

Then I knew exactly what to do. I wrote the following letter: "Dear Boys, I know you will be very sad and disappointed that you didn't receive Evil Knievel this Christmas. I had an accident while traveling across the country delivering toys to the children of the world. Your two Evil Knievel dolls fell out of my sleigh and dropped down a chimney. But I think you will be happy to learn that the chimney was at an orphanage and two little boys will be happy this morning with your toys. I hope you will understand and forgive me."

"Love, Santa Claus"

On Christmas morning, the boys rushed to the tree where they found the message. They read the letter several times. One child had a huge tear on his cheek that I will never forget. Then they smiled and one said, "Well, that's all right; we have lots of other toys." The other answered, "Yes and I'm glad an orphan has Evil Knievel because he will love him and that may be the only toy he gets today."

That was the happiest gift I ever had.

Merry Christmas!

Christmas Shopping Interferences

Christmas shopping started this year with a bang and a bizarre trip. For several years, my friend, Sue, and I have attended Christmas Village in Nashville, shopping, enjoying a good dinner and spending the night. The next day is followed by another shopping trip, a leisurely lunch and then we come home.

I should have known that this year would be different when I learned that my husband had to catch an early plane at the Nashville airport and we left home at 6 AM. (It has always been my opinion that nothing good starts at 6 AM)

When we were in the car, my husband asked me if I remembered that both our sons had doctor's appointments in Nashville the next day. The appointments had been made six months before, so how was I supposed to remember that? After he broke the news to me, he boarded a plane and I went in search of a telephone to try to change the appointments or make some arrangements to get the boys to Nashville. All that confusion just blew my day at the start.

Naturally, it was impossible for the doctor to work in two boys for five minutes each on some other day in the near future. The next opening was late March. After numerous phone calls, some local and some long distance, Sue and I devised the plan to have the boys come to Nashville on a bus the next day. Then we went shopping at Christmas village where we walked for nine hours around and around to the various booths.

Sue immediately saw a flower arrangement she wanted, but she hesitated for three minutes and a nasty old lady grabbed it and bought it on the spot then Sue's day was shot also. (All day she lamented over that flower arrangement.) By evening both of us were crippled from all that walking so we called it a day and joined my aunt for dinner.

The next morning in Tullahoma, two sleepy boys arose at 5 AM and dressed. At 6 AM, they had a cold breakfast and at 7 AM, they boarded a vintage bus for Nashville. By 7:30, they stopped in Manchester and decided to get a stack and almost missed the bus. (One stop on that short trip and they got off the bus and were almost left at the station.) They arrived in a sleepy and cross mood.

We decided on a fast shopping trip to a unique store (about the size of a minibar) which was loaded with merchandise. To add to the crowd and confusion, there was a television crew with all their cameras filming Christmas shoppers for a December program. I was running through the store tripping over camera cords while my son was trying to get himself on the television show. He was selected to try on coats for the show. Not wanting to be on television myself, I hid under the coat rack and whispered in a stage voice. "Fix your hair, take off your cap, smile, don't be nervous, and look natural!" The lady doing the show thought she had encountered a talking clothes rack until my son said, "It's only my mom calling out instructions."

Like most shoppers we stayed too long at the store and I made a frantic drive to the doctor's office only to wait one hour before we were called in.

With the appointment behind us, we joined Sue, her mother and her mother's dog for the trip home. The car was so loaded we couldn't see out the back. We looked like a band of gypsies who were moving to another location.

Of course, the boys became hungry just as we got out of town so we stopped at a little cafe, which usually only had fast food service, to find that one man alone had showed up for work that day and the restaurant was full. There was nothing fast about that meal.

We went the last stretch of the way with the dog alternating between wanting to ride in the front seat and sniffing at a package in the backseat containing a "Puppy Christmas Wreath" complete with dog bones and toys.

Unloading that car was like trying to move a mountain. It was dark, cold and we had to unload our wooden angels, wreaths, baskets, candy, crystal and a flyswatter (which was used to control the dog.) All and all, I must say that the dog was the most adaptable traveler we had, except for Sue's mother. The rest of us were exhausted and overwrought.

If my shopping trips continue like this I won't be here for Christmas. Before December 25, I will have been certified as a "basket case".

Christmas Stories

Christmas is over and hopefully all children everywhere are happy. Parents have collapsed from fatigue but that, too, is part of the holiday season.

Our family reviewed some amusing stories of holidays we shared in the past. As we were trimming the Christmas tree, one of the boys said, "Now this is a pretty tree." Another remarked, "I think all our trees have been nice." Then we all broke into laughter when we remembered the year that we had the oddest tree ever grown.

Selecting the tree, in my opinion, should be a family tradition. When the children were young, there was no problem. As they grew older, each person wanted a different tree. Often we ended up with hurt feelings, pouting or sometimes driving all over town to find a tree which suited all of us.

One year my husband secretly decided to "take matters into his own hands." All of us crammed into the car to look for a tree. At the first place we arrived, my husband immediately jumped out of the car. Before we could reach him, he shouted "I've found the tree" and paid for it. That tree was absolutely the first one he saw and he was determined not to have the usual hassle of the past.

When we got home, we were horrified to see that our tree was so bent and slanted it looked like "The Leaning Tower of Pisa." It was also the oddity of the neighborhood. People would laugh and say, "Have you seen the Bowman's Christmas tree this year?"

The next story took place in my childhood when my elderly great-uncle Joe came for Christmas dinner. Mother had made a tray of tiny, delicious sandwiches decorated with parsley and relishes.

When we started setting the buffet table, no one could find the sandwiches. The hot dishes were getting cold as we all searched. Uncle Joe calmly talked while the rest of us ran through the house looking for the sandwich tray. We decided finally to forget that tray and start eating.

When Uncle Joe got up to enter the dining room, there was the tray of sandwiches in his chair and he had been sitting on them all the time.

So we have had a leaning tree and flat sandwiches but a big dose of laughter of happy memories.

Crash Diets

My husband and I have just finished a three day "crash" diet. Now, I know why some diets are called that. The victim literally falls over from hunger and crashes on the floor. This diet must've been made by a bunch of crazy maniacs who love to suffer. Our son obtained a copy from some wrestlers in a health spa in Nashville. I hope he has found some new friends by now because those guys are "sickos."

The first day wasn't bad except for the dry toast and peanut butter for breakfast. We had 900 calories that day. The second day was 800 calories which consisted of a bazaar combination of food. I spent that day walking back and forth in the kitchen and reading the diet just to be sure that I hadn't overlooked something and I was so weak that the distance from the family room to the kitchen was all I could manage to walk.

The second day my husband had lost 5 pounds. I didn't have the energy to get to the scales. Both of us were so irritable that the boys offered to get us a pizza and the television commercials bothered me. I was seeing hamburgers on the screen and I would shout, "Change that channel immediately!"

The third and last day was a killer. We got one fourth of a cup of cottage cheese and four crackers for lunch. I counted those crackers over and over again to be sure that I had four. Then I checked the diet again to see if I had misread it; perhaps it called for five. (This was the 600 calorie day.) In addition to our weakness and irritability, I developed headaches and stomach disorders. (Is it any wonder?) I kept saying, "This diet is hazardous to our health." My husband, a disciplined person, said, "This is our last day and our goal is 10 pounds. Surely, you can finish." However, he wasn't so thrilled to see our dinner for that last night.

We were allowed ¼ cup of tuna fish, cauliflower and beets. If there is anything in the world he does not like it is tuna fish. Actually, I like it so I was rather superior and said, "After all, this is our last day. Surely you can finish." When he came home from work, the boys were rushing out the door "Where are you going?" He asked. "Out to eat cheeseburgers and French fries." They answered. Then I said, "I couldn't stand it. "How can I fix their meals and actually watch them eat? So I gave them some money and told them to get lost." He smiled sadly and I knew that he understood.

Then, he asked me an extraordinary question. "Can you make a casserole with tuna fish, cauliflower and beets?" (I know he had had gone over the edge at that point.) "Just rest until I get our food ready," I suggested.

The next morning he said, "I just lost 6 pounds. How about you?" "I'm too weak to weigh-in, barely have enough strength to get to the kitchen and fix us a decent breakfast," I answered.

The next time our son recommends a diet to us, I am going to throw it away before my husband sees the copy.

December Memories

December is a sentimental month for our family. Besides Christmas, we celebrate three birthdays and an anniversary. In this column, I would like to pay tribute to the birthday group and relate a few remembrances of the past.

Our son, Steve, will be 23 years old on December 23. He is the oldest son and the serious one with the right sense of humor.

Many years ago, we went to Disney World for vacation and my husband was not able to go. My aunt and I took the children and we noticed that Steve helped us in a mature way by doing the jobs that Dad would've done. He packed and unpacked the car all along the way. He looked after his younger brothers and was generally a wonderful help to us. One evening, after our arrival in Florida, after all day at the park, I decided to go back to Disney World and take the youngest son, Sam. Everyone else was exhausted and decided not to go. Steve told me what time to catch the last tram and motel bus back, what time Disney World closed and gave me more instructions that his dad would if he had been there.

Well, I had young Sam with me and we were having so much fun that we forgot to catch an earlier tram/bus back to the motel. We finally took the last tram which was to take us to the motel bus site. And the tram broke down. But after 15 minutes, we were on our way again and I was happy to discover that the motel bus had waited for us. But my shock came when I arrived at the motel. There was Steve standing in front, pacing back and forth and talking to the doorman.

I got off the bus with a Mini Mouse watch on my wrist and a banner in my hand and little Sam was carrying a large stuffed Donald Duck. We were all smiles and full of the excitement of the evening. Steve walked over to me and proceeded to tell me that he thought we had been locked up for the night in Disney World and he was planning to call the authorities. Also, that I wasn't responsible to take a small child if I didn't know what time to come back. He saw my new watch and remarked, "Why didn't you buy a Mickey Mouse hat with the big ears and wear that too?" I was amused and he was furious and he gave a heated report to his Dad back home. Later, I learned that he had been pacing the lobby and entrance for hours (meeting every bus) and finally had told the doorman that he was waiting for his mother and baby brother that his mother was a "little crazy" and had no sense of time.

Now, Steve has grown into a fine young man with the same drive, temper, intensity and maturity that he showed that evening when he made himself responsible for his "crazy mother."

Then there is Sam, the youngest, who is 16 years old today, December 21. Sam has a serious side also but he likes to pull pranks on the family. His latest and most serious was a letter he typed (perfect typing – no mistakes) which he intended for me and I was to think the letter was from Auburn High School. This was in late May of this year and the letter informed me that Jim, our middle son, then a senior would not graduate. I was told to contact the school immediately. I did! I was in hysterics. Actually, Sam did not give me the letter but I found it in the school annual. However, it was so authentic looking that I never dreamed it was not real. Sam's little joke added more gray hairs to my head and nearly devastated me. But that's a memory I will never forget and today I can finally see the humor behind the letter.

Last but not least my husband, Sam, celebrated a birthday on December 10 and he is the man who has helped me live through all the above episodes all these years. He has been the rock of my existence and the strong shoulder to lean on.

To my husband, Sam, and my sons, Steve and Sam, I say "Happy Birthday" and I hope that I can bring you just have as much joy as you all have brought to me.

(Note: I learned that another "famous person" also celebrated a birthday on December 10 so I salute Tony Carter of Glen Dean Drug Store and give him my best wishes.)

And to you friends, Merry Christmas to all of you!!!!

Don't Block TV During Football Games

There has long been a silent understanding among women that no one interferes while I man is watching a football game. However, I am reminded of a true story I read three years ago about a woman who blocked the television set and was shot and killed.

I really couldn't believe the article until I reread it several times. A 56 year old man shot and killed his 56 year old girlfriend because she was tired of football and stood between him and the television set during the telecast of the Arkansas -Texas game.

According to the newspaper account, he warned her several times to get out of the way and threatened to get his shotgun.

I was discussing this with some friends and one said, "I remember that game. It was a good one."

How many women do you think have threatened to do that very thing? I know I have. But I learned years ago (when my husband watched a football game on television during our wedding reception) that I could not compete with football. And I could not get sick, have a baby or encounter any emergency during a game. Nevertheless, until I read that article, I had thought of standing in front of the television set and blocking the view just to get someone to talk to me.

Well now I have certainly reconsidered my position and will never try that tactic. There must be a safer way to get someone's attention-like starting a fire or setting off the burglar alarm. I really don't find this absolute an insult but I have no intention of ever again even walking in front of a television set during a football game.

All you women out there, be warned!!

Double Coupon Day

A reader suggested this column while we were shopping at the grocery on double coupon day. Double coupon day is to the housewife what the State Fair is to children.

With rising grocery prices and inflation everywhere, some groceries give double the value of coupons on a certain day. That day almost puts the joy back into grocery shopping. When you drive by a grocery store and can find no parking place and see women rushing inside with envelops full of coupons and a grocery list 18 inches long, you know you have hit the right place on double coupon day.

To some shoppers, it is an art. My mother has been clipping out coupons for years (and sharing them with me-for which I'm thankful.) She has made a science out of it and can always match her items with her coupons.

Mother was telling me that she heard of a woman who bought groceries totaling over $100 and with her coupons. She only paid something like $3. (Can you imagine the poor shopper behind that lady in the line?) My father says that mother is so deft with her coupons that he thinks if she used them all at once on a grocery shopping trip, the store would actually owe her money. He's probably right.

In a way, it's a challenge and a game. You wander through a store looking for coupon items that you need and meet some interesting people. After a while, you start helping each other and exchanging coupons. I'll bet some permanent friendships are made that way.

Hopefully, shoppers will be more organized than one of my friends who spent nearly an hour sorting her coupons and making her grocery list using the brand names for which she had the coupons. Then she put her list and all those coupons in a folder and went to the grocery. After an hour and a half of shopping, she happily went to the checkout counter with the knowledge that she had saved a great deal of money. After methodically checking the coupons, the checker told her that one third of the coupons had expired but she still had quite a lot which were current. "Well," my friend said, "that's all right. I'll still come out ahead because I'm shopping on double coupon day."

The checker was very sympathetic when she informed my friend that double coupon day was the day before and would she like to use the coupons today or wait until next week when double coupon day came around again? Have you ever see a grown woman sobbing over a check-out counter in a grocery with 30 customers looking on?

Easter Faith of a Child

With Easter approaching I remember this year, as I have in all the years passed, of the faith and belief of a small child. Since Easter is a joyous Christian holiday which also involves faith and hope, I don't think it is irreligious to associate the faith of a child in the Easter Bunny with that faith that Christians have on Easter morning.

A child's mind can accept more complicated beliefs on faith alone then can the mind of an adult. This incident involves one of my sons when he was very young and his world was bounded by Santa Claus, the Easter Bunny and all the legends our children embrace.

On that Easter weekend many years ago, we were visiting my aunt and uncle in Nashville, Tennessee. All that week we had talked of the Easter Bunny, a basket full of candy eggs, an Easter egg hunt and church service on Easter morning with the white lilies filling the church.

My son became more excited as each day passed; however, he could not imagine how a bunny could carry so many baskets to children all over the world. It seemed an impossible task – yet he wanted to believe.

We had dyed and decorated eggs together but he wanted to leave some lettuce and carrots outside for the Easter Bunny. He just knew the bunny would have had a long and tiring trip and would be hungry. He reasoned that unless people left snacks along the way, the bunny wouldn't be able to cover all his territory before Easter morning.

The night before Easter my son couldn't sleep. He kept listening for sounds outside and rushing to the window. When he said his prayers, he asked that the bunny have a safe trip. After he had checked the supply of lettuce and carrots outside for the 3rd time. He finally settled down and fell asleep.

Early on Easter morning when my uncle went to the window, he saw a beautiful, plump, brown rabbit running through the yard. He rushed to awaken my son and carried him to the window. The child's eyes sparkled with excitement and he kept saying over and over, "He did come, he did come after all." He rushed outside and found the lettuce and carrots gone but in their place was an Easter basket with candy eggs, jelly beans and a small toy rabbit.

For many years, he talked of that Easter morning and marveled that he was lucky enough to actually see the Easter Bunny on his rounds. It was a little lesson in faith which made a big impact on a child's mind. He had believed and it had come true.

Energy Director

There was a job vacancy in our house so we appointed one of the boys to be energy director. With the costly utility bills today, it was worth the price to have someone check on lights, television sets, radios and doors left open.

The energy director (son Jim) was equipped with a notebook and pencil. He was to issue citations to offenders in the family. The offender, after three citations, would be required to pay any fine.

I was the first person cited--light left on in the bedroom. My husband was the second offender to be caught. He left the room briefly while watching television and was handed a citation when he returned. (The other children warned us that we were giving too much power to this child.)

This kid really took his job seriously. He patrolled the house like a Secret Service Agent. But he was doing a good job so we couldn't complain.

However, one evening he became too over-zealous with his authority. After everyone had gone to bed, I heard him walking in the hallway. I thought he had gone for a glass of water. The family awoke at 5 AM, freezing. My husband ran to the thermostat thinking something had happened to the heating system. The thermostat was set below 50°- the lowest setting.

After we all thawed out, we had a serious discussion with the director. He explained that he had heard the previous night was to be the coldest this winter and he knew we would be using too much electricity so he turned the thermostat down. (The President could sure use this kid in Washington.)

When he realized that his salary would stop if he lost his clients by freezing them to death, he agreed to leave the thermostat alone and carry on with his other duties of just issuing citations.

Exercising

Have you ever noticed how people (especially men) go crazy over physical exercise when they are nearing 40? If you don't believe me, look out the window at the joggers and don't get in their way unless you enjoy being run down.

Check the tennis courts, bicycle routes, golf courses and especially the hospitals. The great race is on to rehabilitate the middle-aged body.

Personally, my efforts to revive myself have all led to disaster-physically and financially. I first tried the gentle sport of swimming. I fell beside the pool and broke my toe. The doctor was amused but my husband wasn't when he got the bill. I really blame my husband for all this anyway so he can just pay the bill without comment.

He was the one who took told me I was flabby and my muscles didn't have much longer unless I started to "shaped up."

I tried tennis and had a heat stroke the first day. After that, no one would approach the tennis court when I was around.

My family thought my efforts were becoming so funny that I got mad and dug my old bicycle out of the garage. When I started down the road, three cars stopped to ask if I needed help. That angered me so much but I found the highest hill in the town. (Even a professional mountain climber would avoid that one!)

I walked my bike up that hill and rested, took the big step and started to race down. My dog couldn't keep up with me. I soared through the air like Evil Knievel! I couldn't stop the bicycle once I started down. I was going so fast I could hardly stay on. I was trying to decide if I should hit a car or a ditch to stop myself when I ran into a tree.

The broken leg cost about $200 and mercifully got me out of circulation for a while. All this time while I am being attended by numerous doctors and hospitals, my husband was insisting that I just haven't found the right sport yet. He is running, doing push-ups and playing 18 holes of golf while I lie around and get exhausted watching him.

After I got out of my leg cast, I took up golf. I liked that for a week then one day when I was teeing off, I snapped something in my back. I was in traction for two weeks and people were actually walking by my hospital room and pointing at me. I think I was on the verge of getting into the Guinness Book of World Records.

On the last day of my hospital stay for the back injury, my husband found me reading a book on "Techniques of Skydiving."

"I've been thinking honey," he said. "Why don't you enroll in that ceramics class? You've always wanted to take ceramics and make your own canister set."

"No." I firmly insisted (after all, he started the whole thing.) "I want to pursue my career in sports."

"What career," he shouted. "All you've done is break yourself up and stay in the hospital. Do you realize how long it has been since we've had a home-cooked meal or had someone wash our clothes for us?"

"But I love sports so much," I persisted. "And it's so good for me to exercise and not get flabby."

"Listen to me," he screamed. "The insurance company is going to cancel us because of you. Improve your mind by taking courses and making your own canister set. Anything, just leave sports to the rest of us. "Also, a salesman from the cemetery called today about plots for us. He's been reading the paper and has seen your name in the hospital news so many times lately that he thought we might be in the market for plots. How do you think that made me feel, honey?"

I don't know how he felt but I was overjoyed. My canister set's nearly completed now.

Father's Day

A father is often the least appreciated person in the family. Everyone depends upon him but all too often we neglect to say "Thank You."

I, too, am guilty of forgetting to thank my husband for the important role he has played in my life and the lives of our three sons.

And my own father deserves special praise for the love he has given me all these years. (Both men really deserve a medal for putting up with me.) This Sunday, I hope you will thank the man who cared for your children, who has touched your life and left it better for his presence.

So today, I dedicate this column to fathers everywhere in honor of Father's Day.

A father is wisdom when tempers are flying and mother is too emotional to handle the situation. A father is taller and stronger than anyone else in the world when a little child is looking up to him.

God gave fathers the strength to stand firm and broad shoulders to lean on.

When an emergency arises, only a father can keep that steel control while he is silently praying for everything to be all right. Everyone else is looking to him for comfort and strength. No one knows how frightened and insecure he feels because he doesn't show it.

Only a father can have the patience and enjoyment of fishing with his son, teaching him to play ball, admiring his daughter's new dress (even though he is paying for it,) checking out her date in a polite way (while he prays that she will be safe)and still enjoy being a father.

Only a father can smile with pride when his son passes down a pair of outgrown shoes to dad. He feels the same pride when he is told that his daughter is smart as well as pretty. Being a father is a 24 hour a day job, seven days a week (no vacations.) Wherever he is, across town, across state, across the world, a father is still in his child's heart and he feels the same.

A father suffers, rejoices and grows with his children.

As the years pass, a father watches his children grow and work toward achievements. When the awards are presented, only a father stands tall with pride and has a special misty, wishful gleam in his eyes.

He sees his son, an extension of himself, taking a faltering step toward adulthood. Although he knows he is losing a part of his little boy, he knows with joy that he is raising a man.

A father sees his little girl as a fragile, tiny thing who needs his constant protection. As the years go by, that delicate little flowers starts to show a will of her own. Her father is baffled but amused.

The day comes when her father realizes that his daughter is a woman. His pride in her is only diminished by the fact that she will leave. He will have to hand her over to another man someday. But when that day arrives, her daddy will look at her through tear filled eyes and see a young woman ready to start her life. Then he will know that he hasn't lost her-will never lose her.

From little boys and girls-to men and women-a father has lived every moment. And so the process of life goes on.

Hair Dressers Control Women's Lives

It recently occurred to be while sitting under the hair dryer at the beauty parlor that no one realizes the power and control which hairdressers have over women's lives. It is my opinion that hairdressers (with babysitters being a close second) rule the world.

During the hour and a half that I spend at the beauty salon, the phone rings constantly with messages about changing appointments, requests for appointments and pleas to "work in" customers for special occasions.

My own husband has said that all our married life the entire family schedule has revolved around my beauty parlor appointments. I think that's an unfair remark but he did cite some strong examples to prove his case.

He mentioned the time during a snowstorm when I put my car in neutral and literally pushed it down the driveway and jumped in to get to the beauty parlor for my regular appointment. Yet, earlier I had refused to walk to the mailbox because of the weather.

And he reminded me of the time when we were expecting our third child and I wanted to look "nice" after the baby was born. The last three weeks before the baby's birth, I went to the beauty parlor on Monday, Wednesday and Friday. "Just in case." When our son was born, I remarked how lucky it was that I had recently had my hair fixed. "How does luck get into this" my husband asked, "when you lived in that beauty parlor for the last month?"

And I have always tried to adhere to the unwritten rules of a good customer. Always give notice in advance when breaking or changing an appointment. If you don't show up at your regular time without a call, don't expect to have your name on the appointment book in the future. Always offer to pay when you have missed an appointment which could have been filled from the waiting list.

If you have an emergency and must leave town or the state, have a friend break your appointment or call long distance. Hairdressers are not in the business for fun and relaxation and they enjoy eating three meals a day too.

If you follow these rules, (which is just courtesy,) you will always be in good standing, look decent from the brow up and enjoy years of a good friendship and relationship with that very important hairdresser who, after all, knows you almost as well is your own family.

Happy Thanksgiving to All

It's Thanksgiving again and time for families to gather for their traditional meal and most importantly to give thanks for their blessings.

I have been blessed many times and in many ways but one which will sound trivial is very important to me. I have never had to cook the turkey! Well, I finally admitted it publicly. Now the truth is out in the open.

In past years, we have either been invited to family dinners or had our favorite cook with us—my aunt. She is 75 years young and knows in her heart that I am not intelligent enough to cook a turkey. Wherever we live, she comes to fix the Thanksgiving dinner. One year she was absent and I attempted a turkey roll which wasn't too successful. I think she heard the reports of that meal and decided that my family was being deprived of the traditional Thanksgiving and she was right.

Each year she arrives with grocery bags filled with products to prepare the items which are on her Thanksgiving Day menu. One time she even brought the frozen turkey in a cooler. And what a feast we enjoyed! She cooks all the evening before and puts the turkey in the oven to bake slowly overnight. The next morning she is up early to continue cooking and roll out her homemade rolls. (Yes, I do help but she says I am a hindrance in the kitchen.)

It suddenly occurred to me last year that she is a tradition and without her with us, Thanksgiving and Christmas would arrive with a thud.

Her arrival is always exciting because we all love her and enjoy her visits. And when she comes from Nashville, she has her car packed to overflowing with Thanksgiving items, Christmas items, gifts and the genuine cheer and happiness that she radiates.

So, this Thanksgiving our family wants to give thanks for our many blessings of life, our sons, our love as a family and for Aunt Punk who has blessed our lives by her existence and her love.

And may God richly bless each one of you on this special occasion. Happy Thanksgiving!!

High School Graduation

One of the most typical experiences in mixed emotions which parents have to face is the high school graduation of their child. I know the emotion is strong in the father and often he cannot express it openly but in this column today, I am speaking primarily from a mother's point of view.

Forgive the sentimentality but I have a son (my first child) who is graduating in a few days. His senior friends also are graduating and I know how many of their mothers are feeling just as I—a little lost. It's very much like the first day we sent them to school. We sat home all day thinking about them, wondering what they were doing. Were they homesick? What were they eating for lunch? Did the teacher like them and did she understand them? In most cases (as was my experience), the child weathered the day wonderfully but the mother was devastated.

And now, after all those years from the 1st grade through the 12th, we mothers are again facing the same emotions. It is a selfish feeling and we are ashamed of it. We know that we should feel pride and happiness that we have raised and prepared these young people to face this day. Proud that they are prepared to go on to another phase of their lives. Yet for all our self-scolding there remains an empty, sad feeling that a part of our child is being lost forever to us.

As these young people stand in line waiting for their diplomas, each mother sees the entire life of her child flash through their mind and heart. We remember the day he (or she) was born, his childhood, and the funny, childish things he said and did. Many memories are crowded into those few minutes.

Suddenly you ask yourself, "Where did the years go? Was I always there when I was needed? Did I do everything I should to the make this child happy and yes, help him grow into a good person? Did I teach him self-reliance, the right values, to be his own person and to think for himself?"

"Did we talk enough and did I listen? What more could I have done to get this child-no-this young adult, ready for a new sort of life.

Realizing that his life will change with a new environment, new friends, new experiences, we know that our life too, will be different. There will be an empty place and empty bed in the house. No matter how many children we have, all are different and unique personalities. One special personality will be away, not experiencing our daily routine as he has for so many years. Of course, we pray will be a part of his new life although forced to do so from a distance.

Even for those graduates who stay at home either to start work or to continue their education, it will never be quite the same. Gone are the high school days which were filled with so many experiences and which will be days to remember but never to be lived again in the same way.

That part of the graduating class leaving town will scatter to various parts of the country. Each student will be following his own path in his own way perhaps to meet again for reunions.

We are proud that these young adults have come to this day. We are grateful that we were allowed to have them in our lives for this long. We just had not realized-until this moment-that our child was this grown-up, this adult ready to take that new step. The full impact of this fact hits us squarely in the face when we first see that graduating cap and gown.

To you mothers who still have young children, enjoy every valuable moment with them. (And I know some moments are very trying.) They will, indeed, grow up before you notice it or accept it.

To all you young people who are graduating in this class and especially to my own son, Steve, I wish you Godspeed. Remember that home is in the heart. It will always be there. Your room, your bed, your place at the table and your special place in our life will never be taken from you.

Home, and all that it means to you personally, is waiting for your return and the door will always be open to you.

I Failed My Test

A mother always wonders what her children would do without her-would they missed her?-would they eat properly?-would they behave any better in her absence? I have always thought if a parent could answer these questions positively, then the mother had done a good job with the children.

Recently, I was hospitalized and this experiment was put to a test. I failed! On a scale of 1 to 10, I scored a -1 as a mother. It was a shock!

Before I left for the hospital, my children asked, "What will we eat while you are gone?" (Not, "Will you get along all right after surgery?") "Who will take us where we need to go? Be sure to leave us enough money." (That should have been my first indication of where I stood in their opinion.)

They had a lovely young lady named Cindy (not her real name) staying with them. After her time here, I think Cindy has given up any wish for marriage and a family. It's a shame that we shattered the dream of such a nice person.

One of the boys became slightly ill and demanded to be taken to the doctor at 5:30 AM. The boys argued constantly over trivial matters and one made constant long distance phone calls to the hospital (whenever Cindy was out of the room.) He wanted to tell me how awful his brother was treating him.

This child also called Cindy at work in the afternoons with little "tricks" like telling her he was running away from home and pretending he was crying from his brother's cruelty. She had more patience and endurance than me. Personally, I would have left those kids high and dry and not given them any phone numbers where they could find me! Cindy was so loyal that she even worried that I was be upset.

When we arrived home, my aunt (a nurse) gave them a 24 hour warning to either straighten up or we (she and I) were packing to leave them. That got their attention! Finally.

Even though I failed the mother test, I have decided that I will not ever willingly submit to this test again by giving them another chance. After all, one has to know when to accept one's losses and go on.

The only regret is that we have dashed the dreams and hopes of us such a nice person like Cindy who thought that children, home, a fireside and family pets were the great American dream. (I thought the same thing too, at her age.) Now, we may have removed completely one lovely person from the marriage and children market. More's the pity!

Income Tax Time

It's income tax time which is known in our house as DDIM Day (Danger Dad is Mad.) I dreaded it every year.

The children are smart - they disappear for most of the time. I quietly creep around the house smiling and fixing my husband's favorite meals. I speak only when spoken to (can't break his concentration) and then I tried to make little jokes hoping he will chuckle or possibly smile just to break tension, but on The DDIM Day, he's not in a chuckling mood.

Trying to help, I search for deductions that he may have overlooked. I mentioned the dog and his vet bills, his collar and rabies tag. Also, I pointed out the tropical fish, the goldfish, their aquarium, fishbowls, equipment and food costs for them. My husband just stared at me with a strange look and shook his head.

One of the children presented his drugstore receipts for anti-blemish soap and anti-acne face pads. (Dad didn't appreciate that.) Another child did his part by showing all the tubes of toothpaste he had used to prevent cavities.

Another suggested we try to figure out how much we have spent this past year on food for stray pets. (Personally, I thought that was a novel idea but my husband informed us that the IRS doesn't accept novel ideas.)

Things were quite tense while dad worked at his desk with forms, papers, receipts and at big headache.

Even our dog MacArthur, who had been watching us with great interest, got into the spirit of things. He is very intelligent and was aware that we were bringing all sorts of odd items to my husband's desk so Mac brought an old, dried bone and put it at my husband's feet. (Perhaps he thought we were celebrating a birthday.) Mac then found a comfortable spot beside the desk, kept a faithful vigil beside my husband just like the pictures portraying the dog as man's best friend.

However, poor MacArthur got a shock when my husband accidentally rolled over the dog's foot with his desk chair. That shattered the image of man and his faithful dog because Mac took off for another part of the house.

I have a feeling that my husband will be on his own next year because Mac will not offer to help or comfort.

Incredible Microwave Experiences

My experiences with the microwave oven should be sent in to "That's Incredible." Note that I say "my experiences," not my recipes nor tips for greater efficiency using the microwave.

Two major mistakes were made at the time of purchase. First, I neither enrolled in a microwave school nor had my IQ tested and secondly, I selected an oven that looks like a computer. Nothing is simple on this microwave like high and low settings and on and off buttons. No, this big oven stares at me and defies me to push buttons 0 through 9 and any of the following: Oven Temp, Micro-Convec Temp and Time, Micro-Control Temp and Time, Preheat, Convec Temp and Time, Clear, Start, Stop, Program Defrost, Pause, Memory Recall and Time of Day. (Yes, it even has a clock on it which blinks widely and constantly until reset if we have one second of power failure.)

It is hard to believe that I so over estimated my intelligence that I even allowed this oven to be brought into my home. But I was eager and willing to learn – or so I thought. For five days, I just looked at the microwave and thought of radiation. The sixth day, I boiled a cup of water and recorded the page number for water in the cookbook. Then, I ventured to bacon and was successful. Gaining courage, I over microwaved 10 hot dogs.

When I had overcome that hot dog disaster, I heated an egg casserole and heard the eggs hit the oven door and swirled around everywhere except in the dish. My confidence vanished and I went back to boiling water again.

The chicken pot pie was a disaster of my entire cooking career. Yes, I transferred the pie to a micro dish. I served it to my husband who looked puzzled and said there was nothing inside between the two crusts - - nothing! I went back to the oven and there was no sign of an explosion. Could the filling in the pie have been left out at the factory? Could it just have vanished without a trace? To this day, I do not have an answer. The only clue I ever got was at a microwave demonstration and the instructor said that pot pies did not cooked well in the microwave. Her opinion, she said. (Yeah, tell me about it.)

Now, I have transferred the blame to the microwave cook book which does not follow through with adequate instructions. A book should not leave the reader with its instructions for water, bacon, potatoes and then say, "Now, you're on your own." Some of us experience fear and nervousness when we read parting words like that.

After seven month as a microwave owner I graduated to defrost. After some successful attempts, I was feeling my power and started defrosting. I had so much fun that I defrosted and partially cooked half of the meat in the freezer.

At that point my family held a meeting and asked me to stop reading the cookbook. They requested that I enroll in a microwave cooking school and learn step-by-step how to use this oven properly.

But I redeemed myself with peanut brittle! There was a nifty and fast recipe for peanut brittle which I mastered from just one session at the microwave demonstration.

The first evening I made it, I pointed to a sign on all the doors: "Fresh homemade peanut brittle served here." Everyone was impressed. I should have known that one cannot live on past glories. A few minutes later after a hectic day, my husband came home expecting a good, hot dinner. When I presented him with peanut brittle, I thought he was going to put me in the microwave. That just shows you how fickle people are and how fleeting is our success in this world.

At this moment, I am on my way to microwave cooking class. If I am lucky, there may be more on the table tonight than peanut brittle. Remember, I said "If."

It's Still a Man's World

Sorry ladies, but it's still a man's world! Now that I have your attention, I will explain that statement.

In many columns, I have addressed the issue concerning the plight of the mother – housewife – how she is under appreciated, and misunderstood. In this column, I want to say something for working mothers.

Working mothers hold numerous jobs and many of them are not in the office. When a working mother comes home, her day is just partially over. There are meals to be cooked, clothes to wash, a house to clean, non-driving children to transport to various locations, lunches to prepare for the following day, advice to give, problems to hear and many other duties too numerous to list. While she is attending to these duties, she is planning breakfast for the next morning (even if it means putting out a box of cereal,) planning dinner for the next evening and washing the dinner dishes. This is done after her day at the office. In addition, sometime during the week or weekend she does her grocery shopping for the following week, plans her meals, runs errands like going to the cleaners, the bank, the pharmacy, etc.

I also must add that no matter how long and tiring dad's day is at the office, in most cases he can come home, sit in his favorite chair, relax, read or watch television and come to dinner when it is served. Some husbands and children help with the house chores but some do not. If you are a working mother whose family falls into the "do not" category, then, sorry dear, you are out of luck. And I do mean it when I say sorry. Working mothers carry an additional work load beyond that of the housewife which adds to the description of being underappreciated, underpaid and misunderstood.

As a working mother friend told me (and she said it better that I,) "When you work all day and come home and sit down to read the paper, have a glass of wine and take a warm bath, you can depend upon it that your dinner will not be ready on the table for you because— it's still a man's world.

Jury Duty (Part 1)

For years I have wanted to serve on jury duty but the call never came. My husband was called to serve twice in the two years we lived in Kansas and I was very jealous. During his jury service, I went to court every day and listened to the testimony. When I tried to offer my opinion each evening, he curtly reminded me that he couldn't discuss the case. That was not one of his finer moments.

A friend had been waiting for years and years for her summons. So we decided to campaign together. We cornered attorneys at parties and told them about our excellent qualifications. We told all our friends and asked them to pass along the message. We even made a pact: first one chosen would recommend the other. We did everything except take out an advertisement in the newspaper. (We considered that but decided it would hurt our chances.)

My friend went to outrageous lengths. While listening to some attorneys discuss a difficult case one evening at a dinner party (which she hosted,) she grabbed the first person she saw and started discussing, in a loud voice, the problems of finding intelligent people to serve on a jury. She continued the conversation all evening and each time she discussed jurors, she said that she had never been asked to serve and she wanted to do her civic duty. She was available at a moment's notice. Can you imagine some man talking business in a quiet, confidential manner, while the same lady follows him around repeating the same jury duty conversation to him (I don't think she helped our cause.)

We found a newspaper article about a town in Florida that was so desperate for jurors that people walking by in front of City Hall were literally taken off the street and made to serve. We made hasty plans to move there but our husbands stopped us.

Our last ditch plan was to commit a crime to draw attention to ourselves. We planned to tell the news media the entire story and get sympathy from the public. Two things stopped us: our husbands and the possibility that a criminal would never be selected for jury duty.

Recently, my friend wrote that she had met the district attorney, two judges and six attorneys at a party. (I think she actually crashed a lawyer's convention. She will go to any links.) She smugly wrote that she expects her summons any day, has her bag packed for a long case, a car pool replacement standing by and her family on red alert.

If she gets there first, I hope her summons is for December 23rd. She may be locked up all through Christmas and New Year's Day.

Jury Duty (Part 2)

In a recent column, I described how my friend and I had yearned for years to be called for jury duty. She finally got the first summons (which she sent to me "special delivery" just to spite me.) However, the date she was to report for jury duty was the exact date she and her husband were leaving for a trip to the West Coast so she had to ask to be excused. Her situation had a very undramatic end to a very dramatic campaign and I got to serve first, after all. My day in the sun came with unexpected circumstances.

After a two-week vacation, I arrived home to find a letter stating that I had been summoned for jury duty and was to report that day or face contempt of court charge. The letter had been sent by the sheriff. My mail had been collected and held by a neighbor who didn't realize it was a summons to jury duty.

Immediately, I called the courthouse and explained that I had just received the letter. I was told that the grand jury was to be selected that day so I had missed that chance. However, I was on call for a three month period which meant that I had to report every time a case came up and wait to see if I was selected.

Then the call came. I was elated thinking that I would be selected for a big case and arrive home late every afternoon. I stopped off at the grocery to get some staples and a few items for the week. My grocery trip made me 45 minutes late to the nearby town where court was held. That made a bad impression and I was not selected for that case.

I waited another week and was called again. This time I appeared on time. I was not selected. This happened over and over again. Finally even the judge and the court reporter felt pity for me. Can you imagine how many people shun jury duty? Yet here I was, answering the call every time, sitting for hours watching other people and then being turned away.

I had given up hope when the last case came up. I sat there thinking "This is my last chance." After excusing numerous prospective jurors, I was finally called, questioned by both attorneys and accepted. The court reporter even smiled her congratulations. My greatest thrill was receiving a big badge that said "Juror". I wore it the entire time during my case which lasted two days. My dream had been fulfilled.

My only disappointment occurred after the case was over and my sons refused to let me wear my juror badge around town. They said I looked retarded going everywhere with a big badge like that pinned on my dress.

Oh well, they have no sense of the dramatic. More's the pity!

Just Call Me Housewife

Many people give the title "housewife" a demeaning connotation. Quite frankly, if done properly, it is the most difficult and important job in the world.

Consider the plight of the housewife – mother. She tends to the mess of the children, works inside and sometimes outside the home. Her hours are long and her schedule has to be flexible. If she does not hold a job outside the home, she does not qualify for Social Security benefits overall.

I suppose that "work inside the home" isn't considered work. Washing, ironing, cleaning, driving carpools, mending, finding lost children and sortlng everyone's clean and dirty clothes seems to be a minor job.

In my opinion, it's no wonder that so many women go "daffy", turn to soap operas, runaway or just collapse. It's often not their job that bothers them as much as it is the lack of respect and esteem that goes with the job title "housewife."

How many times when you write "housewife" as your occupation on a credit application does someone say, "Oh, you don't work." There are several ways to handle the situation. You can scream, tear up the application, fling it on the floor, say you work at an unpaid job or answer that you are a secret agent posing as a housewife but can't reveal that information on the application. Under no circumstances do you back down and humble yourself as if your job is of no importance.

Yet in every housewife-mother's life there is an unwritten book in her mind. If she could relate her every day experiences, the public would not believe it.

I know this is true because even my own mother, who raised two children, was unbelieving when she called me last week. I was telling her that the boys had been swimming and had thrown a large, rolled up bundle of towels and swimsuits on the floor. Without looking at the contents, I picked up the bundle and inserted it into the clothes dryer. After 45 minutes of drying, I found among the towels and suits a bottle of hot suntan lotion and two tennis balls. "Why didn't you check before you threw everything into the dryer?" Mother asked. "Mother," I answered, "would you believe that I was also cooking dinner, packing a lunch for one of the boys for the next day and checking on a sick puppy – – – all at the same time?" And frankly, I was in a hurry, I was tired and at that point I didn't care what went into the dryer." "Thank goodness one of the boys wasn't rolled up into the towels," she said. "I think she has forgotten a few things!

Life's Interruptions

When the electricity went off at our house on Saturday morning during the cartoons, I was reminded of an incident several years ago when the adult male population of our country "lost their cool."

Do you recall when a professional football game ran too long on television and the last few minutes of the game were lost to the viewers because the regularly scheduled program, "Heidi," came on as planned?

That caused a furor that disrupted the television stations, the telephone companies and even the nation. Angry viewers flooded the stations with calls and threats. Some enraged sports fans even called the police.

I well remember the uproar at our house. My husband was frantically trying to find out why the game was interrupted, my sons were calling the television station, were tearing up the newspapers trying to find the television schedule and trying to pick up the game on the radio.

It was a madhouse! When poor "Heidi" appeared on the screen, I felt sorry for her because I knew that well-loved story would live in the minds of all football fans as the detested cause of their missing the last few minutes of the game.

A similar incident occurred a few weeks ago but, thank goodness, "Heidi" was not to blame. One part of the town lost its electrical power due to trouble at a substation. Unfortunately, that happened at the same time when "Plastic Man" (a television cartoon character) was in great danger.

The breakfast I was cooking at the time was almost as disastrous as "Plastic Man's" problems. The bacon turned cold and the biscuits that were ready for the oven deflated, stuck to the pan and turned into bricks.

However, I coped better than my little television addicted children. They started calling the electric company (now most people there know how poor "Heidi" felt).

Children were calling us to find out if our television was working. One child wanted to call the police and another was hitting the television set and changing the channels at rapid speed with no power. (I guess he was trying to revive it.)

My husband told the boys, "Calm down and pull yourself together. It's only a program." I reminded him of "Heidi" and the football game and he never said another word.

I think there's a message here somewhere about children and adults reacting the same way. Since I haven't figured it all out yet, I'll settle just to find out if "Plastic Man" survived the dive from the cliff and captured the "Disco Monster."

Little League Can Be Trying

Baseball (from Little League to Senior Babe Ruth) is well underway now for our youngsters. That's the time of the year when the Dr. Jekyll and Mr. Hyde syndrome sets in on parents. The player's families sit in the bleachers and it is there that you can see the transformation of kind, nice people into a screaming, fanatic, opinionated crowd.

When those children walk onto the field, all of us parents are filled with excitement and great expectation. Many of us think there may be some hidden talent – some unrecognized future star – in that group. (Usually, we think that about our own child.)

The pressure of the game isn't half as bad on the players as it is on the parents. The players usually don't feel the pressure from the coach as much as they feel it from their own individual parents.

When the games are one-sided, you can always tell which side is losing that's the bleacher side that is filled with grim, dejected looking parents while the other side is cheering wildly for the victors.

But when the game is close, tempers get short among the crowd. I have heard parents scream at their own children on the field about their bad performance. I have seen fathers rush to the dugout to "talk" to the coach because their son or daughter was not playing enough during the game.

On one occasion, I even heard an older adult coach (the word "adult" is questionable in this case) threaten a teenage assistant coach on the opposing team because one of his young players became confused in the excitement and looked at the opposing teenage coach who was signaling to his third baseman. The confused child tried to run for home and was called out. The older coach accused the young coach of giving the child a signal to run. In fact the young coach was telling his own third baseman to watch his base and home plate.

After the game, the older coach, in front of all the players, threatened the teenage assistant coach with the words: "I'll get you some day, some way." You can imagine the example that set for all the youngsters watching. It was especially disgusting because the young coach – like all other coaches – was giving his time, with no pay, to help out a Little League Team who needed an assistant coach.

Also, It is especially amazing how spectators can see better from the stands than the umpire who is a few feet from the plate. (I'm no exception. I always think I saw the play better – if I disagree with the call – than I can even see my own child in right field.)

Umpires do make mistakes. There's no question about that. In some cases, certain people are not good at umpiring but this is not a criminal offense which requires capital punishment.

As long as we have children, parents and games, I suppose this will continue. But the example set by parents can make a huge impact on their own children.

It's hard to teach sportsmanship to your children when you have to explain "Do as I say and not as I do," because that really doesn't make much sense.

Meet Mr. Dynamic

Every family has one child who can command, get constant attention and locate a parent anywhere. That child is usually the nucleus of the family and a dictator. Yet often this same child is of a sweet disposition, helpful, caring and the one "who gets things done" In the family. Usually he (or she) has to have the last word in every discussion, outlasts the rest of the family and is so sure that his opinion is right he drives you crazy insisting on his "point of view."

In the end, the rest of the family is so exhausted that they agree with him, give in to him or just demand that he shut his mouth. That's the child you should consider sending to law school. Let him badger a jury or his opponent and turn his talent into something constructive.

Because he is the dynamic one, he is able to locate any family member in 5 minutes within the state, in 10 minutes outside the state, and 15 to 20 minutes outside the country. He leaves no stone unturned and convinces operators, receptionists and professional people in all walks of life that his call is so urgent, he must be put through immediately.

Mr. Dynamic has paged me at the grocery store, (once when he was there himself but became separated from me), the beauty parlor, the drycleaners, restaurants, meetings, parties and at friend's homes. There is no place on the face of the earth that I could go where he could not find me. I'm convinced that after I depart this life, he will find a way to send a message to me.

Quite frankly, I have been accused by the children of having this son's same trait so his brothers are not sympathetic to me. They see this as a kind of retribution and revenge which I have deserved for years.

If he forgets his tennis shoes, he doesn't hesitate to call me to bring them even if I am attending a luncheon out of town. If he decided to stop for a hamburger on the way home from school, he would locate me at a board meeting to tell me that he will be late.

I am sure that if I were entertaining the President of the United States and the First Lady and my son had forgotten some item, he would casually call me and ask me to bring it to him. If I couldn't come, he would think to ask the Secret Service to come in my place. He just is that type.

He has just called and has an errand for me. I must go as I can't keep him waiting unless I want to be tracked, traced and paged all over town.

Men Are Packrats Too

Men are always laughing about women saving things and accuse us of never throwing anything away. Well, there's another side to that story as many women know.

For instance, my neighbor tells me that her husband still saves his old hunting clothes and he hasn't gone hunting in years. He refuses to dispose of them in the event that he may, at any moment, decide to go hunting. He also has saved his Navy uniforms which are now about 40 years old.

He is not the exception to the rule. My husband has the same trait although he steadfastly denies it. For years, he has called me a "packrat" because I keep things like old shoes that are out of style, old greeting cards and letters and the dress I wore on our first date. But just ask him about his old tennis jacket (now yellow with age), his high school jacket with a football letter on it and even the old Army uniform which he finally parted with last year.

His attachment to his old clothes was manifested several years ago when he went jogging daily with our son.

After the first week of their jogging trips around the neighborhood, my son quietly approached me and asked to speak to me privately about something important. This is his account: "Mom, Have you seen what dad wears to jog every morning? I can't believe you don't know about it, otherwise, you would find him better clothes. I'm no snob and I realize you don't dress up to jog but what dad wears is so awful that all the neighbors are laughing at us. He wears those old gray sweat pants that he had in college and the elastic is gone. In fact, it has been gone for years. He uses a narrow, brown leather belt, that hasn't been used since I was born, to hold the pants up. I think the belt is an antique. And he wears his old college football jersey."

"Honestly, Mom, we are attacked and followed by dogs every morning. I don't blame the dogs because they've never seen anyone dressed like Dad. Now Dad carries a big stick or golf club to defend us. People actually come out of the house to watch us because of Dad's outfit. It's unreal and the bad part is that he doesn't realize how terrible those clothes look. Can we get him new clothes or a jogging outfit?"

That evening I spoke to my husband about his jogging attire. "Those are perfectly good sweatpants except for the elastic being gone," he said. "That football jersey still has years of wear left." "What's wrong with that narrow belt? Just because it's not in style doesn't matter. This way I get some use out of it."

After much talking, pleading, negotiation and compromise, I asked my son, "Would you settle for a new pair of sweat pants for Dad?" After all, you can't win them all!

Mondays Are Cancelled

I have decided to mark Monday off my calendar. I've always wondered why some people called Mondays, "Blue Monday" or identified Monday as "wash day" but now I know that you cannot expect much from that day of the week.

Over the years, I have noticed that the most rushed days are Mondays. The children are more tired and cross when waking up that day, the clothes have all piled up ready for washing and refused to go away until you take charge of them. In short, Monday is a day in which you clear away the wreckage of the weekend, a day when you don't have anything exciting planned, a day of chores and "catch-up" jobs and the day your house takes its revenge on you.

Really, I should have figured this out sooner as Labor Day always falls on Monday and our worst luck usually comes on Labor Day. For example, on some past Labor Day Mondays, the septic tank overflowed, we had to cancel a long-awaited trip and we were victims of a "speed trap" going to a park in Virginia.

On a recent Monday, I woke up with a headache, my son's tennis shoes had developed big holes in the sides overnight, he had lost a schoolbook and couldn't find his favorite socks. When he told me that his clothes were falling apart, I said, "So am I." He was not amused!

Then he called from school to say he forgot his notebook. I rushed for my coat and car keys to take the book to him. As I put on my coat, two buttons fell off. What else did I expect on a Monday? When I got in the car, my keys were lost. After 20 minutes of searching and repeating to myself, "I hate Monday," I found the keys in the car door.

I shouldn't feel this way about any day in the week but through experience I have built up a prejudice against Mondays. Maybe if I call it by another name I could get through a day calmly. I've thought of calling it, "No Day," "Someday," "Challenge day," and "Doomsday."

Since my attitude is not improving toward Mondays, perhaps I'll just consider having two Tuesdays in every week (Tuesday 1 and Tuesday 2.) That may seem strange to some people who don't know the history behind my Mondays but then, most of us are lucky to remember the month and the year much less the day. I don't think Mondays will be missed.

Mother Driver

In the mind of a teenager, what make makes his (or her) mother suddenly become a reckless, dangerous and incompetent driver? Answer: That teenager has just learned to drive! For the third time, I am a victim who is being unjustly accused of not having sense to drive a car.

I have 25 years of driving experience. No insurance company has ever canceled my policy. I am a licensed driver who has passed the written and driving tests four times in four different states, but suddenly I am a menace on the highway – according to my son.

Once this boy sat calmly in the car, talked in a reasonable tone of voice, napped, read books in the car and was perfectly at ease for 13 years while I drove all over the country. Now, he is nervous, loud, jumpy, frightened and acts in an unstable way while I am driving. I hasten to add that he does not feel the least discomfort or fear when his friends, who are the ripe old age of 16, are driving.

Now, even short trips from home to school are a chore for us both. He watches me as if he expects me to either drop dead at the wheel or leap out of the car. He looks at the centerline in the road and tells me that I am on the wrong side.

He jumps what I pass a car and yells, "You couldn't see far enough ahead to pass." When I turn a corner he shouts, "Stay on your side of the road. You will get us killed." When a car coming from the other direction passes by, he screams, "Move over, move over! You are running that car off the road."

Some of his other comments go like this: "You are going too fast and the car is wobbling all over the road." (We are going 40 miles an hour and the wind is blowing.) "Can't you see? Maybe you need an eye test. Make an appointment today, please." "Just pull over and stop. I will drive. If a policeman stops us, I will explain that you almost got us killed back there and I had to drive us home." "You are not concentrating on your driving. Keep your mind on what you are doing. You passed the street where we were supposed to turn." On and on these comments continue. I tried to be patient as he appears to be serious and genuinely frightened. It's my third time around with this type of behavior. My other sons did the same thing when they learned to drive. In fact, I think I did it too many, many years ago.

As I see it, I have two choices. I can evict him from the car and let him walk or I can wait for that "someday" when he has children and has to teach them how to drive.

Mother Is My Title

I was just thinking of all the times during all these years that I have had the title "Mother" bestowed upon me.

Besides being a mother of three, I have been Team Mother once (baseball), Home Room Mother for three years (school), Carpool Mother, Mother Judge (of more disputes then the Supreme Court has ever handled), Mother Confessor (on-call 24 hours a day), Mother Nurse and head of Mother's Diner which serves fast foods, burned foods and food worth waiting for (when translated that means I haven't started dinner on time.)

Since Mother's Day is almost here, I thought it was only fitting to see how much esteem I have with my family. For years I have read about the annual "Mother of the Year Award" and wondered who nominated her. (I assumed her own children placed her name into nomination.) In the newspapers every year, there is a smiling, gracious lady accepting her award while surrounded by her loving and successful children. That's the American dream come true.

Wondering if I may ever be a candidate (as I do each year), I decided to check out the voters in our house – the grassroots section of voters. There are five not counting the dog. (I am sure of the dog's vote but it would be thrown out.)

The first potential voter I approached told me that my cooking would disqualify me. All those years of gourmet meals and he remembers those few frozen dinners.

The second voters said, "No way, Mom. You are too late getting us at school. I thought that was a real tacky remark since I have been picking up some child for 13 years. Surely that qualified me for some award.

My last hope in the child category said, "Sorry, Mother but you "bug" me too much. In fact, you are the "buggiest" mother I have ever seen."

I thought that was the end of my candidacy until I discussed it with my husband and he gave me a vote of confidence. He said he would have a caucus with the children and then we could assess the results.

After the mini-election at our house, I received two votes – my husband's and my own. I know it's embarrassing to vote for yourself but after all if you don't think you are the best qualified, why run at all?

Well, now that I know where I stand with the children – on quicksand. The award of "Mother of the Year" has eluded me again this time. It would be a humiliating defeat to have your husband place your name into nomination and then have your own children vote against you. In fact, my support was so weak that if the "Wicked Witch of the West" was running against me, she would win.

Needless to say, I bombed out in the family election and never made it to the first primary so I sat down and repeated over and over to myself: "Happy Mother's Day to me, Happy Mother's Day to me…."

Mr. Painter

My path has crossed many interesting people throughout the years and one of them was "Mr. Painter." Actually, he was our house painter with another name but my young sons couldn't pronounce his real name so they dubbed him "Mr. Painter."

He was tall, lanky and rode a motorbike to work with his paint buckets dangling on the back. One of the teenagers in the neighborhood remarked that he was the "coolest" painter he had never seen.

"Mr. Painter" had completed the first story work on our colonial house and then called in that he would be off for a week. His own dog (who hated his motorbike) had attacked him. That dog loved him off the motorbike but not riding it. He had even bought a long dark wig at my garage sale to disguise himself from the dog while he came home on the motorbike. I suspect the poor dog just went over the edge when he saw that scene and attacked.

The first day back at work brought more havoc to "Mr. Painter." He had started the second story of our house and was barely hanging on from the ladder which reached from the garage entrance to the top. It was a hot summer day and my sons were driving me crazy. All morning they had fought each other, complained and cried at the injustices of life. Three boys out of school in the summer heat is explosive anyway you look at it.

Finally about noon, I had had it! I was so angry and nervous that I shouted, "All right boys, March! We are going to the swimming pool to cool off and I don't care whether you want to go or not. You have five minutes to get ready."

I grabbed some towels and suntan lotion then herded them into the car in the basement. Such was my fury that I never gave a thought to "Mr. Painter" who was quietly working on the ladder behind my car. One of the boys complained about something and I shouted, "Quiet, in the car! We are going to have fun if I have to kill you all." With that remark, I started the engine and started backing out of the garage.

After I knocked "Mr. Painter" off the ladder, there was scared silence from the boys. "Mr. Painter" said that he had heard me shouting at the boys (everyone in the neighborhood heard me) and he kept saying to himself, "She surely sees me. She won't back out yet. Mrs. Bowman, Wait, Wait."

Thank goodness he wasn't hurt. Just shaken up. I had jarred his ladder a little but then stopped. He dangled for a while and then dropped off the ladder.

That evening at dinner, my husband explained to the boys that they had almost caused the demise of "Mr. Painter." Then he turned to me and asked if the painting was finished. "No," I answered. "Mr. Painter" has agreed to come back for one more day provided we all are gone from the house, all day, then he plans to retire. He feels safer with his dog.

My Sense of Direction

Some people are just born with a sense of direction and others are not. I was not. Even though I talked all through geography class in the fourth grade and never learned where anything was located, I don't think the instruction would've helped permanently.

When you go through life not knowing where north, south, east, and west are, you should remember two things: your sense of direction is faulty and never get on an interstate.

My case is hopeless because I can't even reverse my directions. Some years ago, I was going to Abington, Virginia from Bristol, Tennessee, (a very short trip - just a few miles.) When I got to Abington, I got confused and couldn't get back to Bristol. When finally I realized I was lost, I had actually gone miles and miles into Virginia in the opposite direction from Bristol.

Another time my husband had a business meeting in St. Louis, Missouri and he foolishly gave me the car to shop. I was to pick him up promptly at 3 PM in a little open area near the interstate. That was during one of the worst winters St. Louis ever had. I started back to get him an hour early but became confused on the interstate (that north, east, west and south problem again.) I finally found him almost frozen. That was, of course, the last time I have been allowed to have the car during a trip.

Those of us who have this direction difficulty usually work out a system to find places. In my case and in the case of my friend, Francis, we select landmarks. Some of my landmarks have been torn down which I consider very inconsiderate, but Francis has had better luck.

Recently, she and her husband were going to visit a relative out-of-state. Francis had been there – by the landmark system – several times but her husband had not.

She instructed her husband to make the first turn at the cow beside a dairy. He passed a huge statue of a cow and turned and asked for the next turn. Francis said, "Turn at the white mule." He wasn't familiar with a place called The White Mule but she had done fine so for so he drove on.

Suddenly Francis shouted, "Turn here." He slammed on the brakes and backed up to turn. As he turned the corner, he saw a real white mule standing in a pasture. If that mule ever moves, Francis will be lost forever.

But as I told her when our husbands were declaring us hopeless, it does take a degree of intelligence to remember all those landmarks.

New Year's Day Belongs to the Men

New Year's Day was created for men. Before you get the wrong impression, let me add that I personally like New Year's Day. But just ask any wife how she spends that day and you will get the same answer 9 times out of 10 - cooking.

Once again this year, I got the message loud and clear when I read a statement in the top corner of The Nashville Tennessean newspaper saying something like "48 hours of football." That's when women rushed to the public library and checked out all the books (in the event they may have time to read.) I imagine some women just ran away from home while others resigned themselves to this once a year fate.

I decided to join in this year and my day went like this: I served what I considered a gourmet brunch which required the use of almost every pan and skillet in the kitchen. After brunch, while I was washing all those pots and pans, I was asked, "When do we eat again?"

That was my cue to start work on the evening meal. I was helped by my family when they took my plant cart, unloaded the plants and brought the cart into the family room where it stood waiting to be filled with food.

During my cooking breaks, I ran in and out of the family room watching snatches of ball games. The real excitement came in the last few seconds of the Alabama - Texas game when the network lost transmission and viewers were left to wonder if Alabama possibly made a comeback. Of all the strange things for the network to do, they put on a rerun of "Good Times" which was not appreciated. In my opinion, it would have been far better to play funeral music as the country was filled with angry, frustrated people who had not tuned into "Good Times." I understand the network received 2 million calls about that.

When I had given up learning the outcome of the Alabama-Texas game, I went back to the kitchen. After all, that food cart was still standing there waiting and empty. Late in the afternoon I loaded the cart with black-eyed peas (for good luck in the New Year), chili, snacks, relishes and a large cheese ball.

When everyone was finished eating and the games were still going on, I returned to the kitchen and started on the dishes again. An hour later, I dragged myself away and mumbled that I was tired and thinking of going to bed. I was answered by looks of shock and surprise. "Why should you be tired when you got to see the football games all day?" I never dignified that question with an answer. Who said it is not still a man's world?

Notes

For years, I have had an obsession about writing notes. I write notes to myself, my family, my friends and to anyone else who cares to read them. Usually they are taped all over the house, the car and my purse.

This habit has caused irritation and embarrassment to members of my family. Even my friends have given me note boards, memo pads and other items which will help me to stay organized without all those unsightly notes. Nothing seems to help.

It is my belief that everyone is eccentric in some way and perhaps this is my odd habit. My husband swears that he has to remove notes from the bathroom mirror to shave. The boys resent my sending notes to school and the doctor and they have been known to tear the notes up before they ever enter the office. (That's why I call and leave my messages over the phone now. Mothers are not completely stupid.)

Actually, my mother has written notes like this since I can remember and I think I inherited the trait from her. However, a neater person cannot be found than my mother and her notes never look cluttered. But she doesn't exactly paper the house with them as I do.

Recently, I realized what a joke and a problem my notes were when my husband was out of town for a few days. Upon his arrival home, we were assigned to drive a group of boys from school to a basketball game 16 miles away. I wrote a long note #1 giving the date, time and all the pertinent facts. When the time was changed, I wrote note #2 explaining that the plans were changed. The third change required me to write addition note #3. When my husband arrived home and saw all those notes, he said, "Do I really have to read all that? Can't you just tell me what the plans are?" (I think he was reading a new book and decided my notes take as long to read as the novel.) When I looked hurt and hinted that he may not understand the schedule unless he read all my messages. He skimmed over them and threw them away.

Strangely enough everything went as planned (according to note #3.) On the way to the game, he remarked, "I have traveled over 1000 miles in two days with no notes. Yet to go 16 miles, you left a total of three notes.

"Don't you think we can live in an orderly manner without all these notes?" he asked, "Well," I answered. "I guess I did get carried away but since you found and noticed my messages, you must have read them all and we did run the carpool for the game according to schedule. We may never know if it was my notes or just luck that brought us through. Will we?" He walked off, shaking his head and muttering, "I give up."

Opposites Attract

Opposites attract. I've heard that all my life and I believe it. It is especially true with friends. Some of my best friends have been perfect and immaculate housekeepers. Anyone who knows me will never mention my name in the same sentence with "Homemaker of the Year."

My brother always said that my idea of spring cleaning was to wash the light switches. I don't like a dirty or messy house but I hate the vacuum cleaner. The last time I used it that monster it threw me all over the house and took off by itself.

When my husband remarked that a house wife of 19 years should be able to handle a simple machine like a vacuum cleaner, I directed it in his path and it ran over his foot. He was lucky he didn't lose a leg. That thing has such strong suction it can pull up a cat. I have spent years working at any job, for anyone, at any wage, just to afford to have someone come in my house and pushed the vacuum.

On the other hand, my friends have shining homes without outside help. I never see them hot and messy nor with a scarf tied around their heads. Everything just looks perfect and sparkling when I enter the front door. I have suffered numerous complexes over this.

Two perfect examples are my friends Pat and Sue. Our friendship has survived only because of two unique experiences. In both cases, I finally found a flaw in their housekeeping. Believe me, I looked for a long time to find an imperfection.

Pat has a large beautiful home filled with French antiques. She also has three children. If those two sentences were written about me, the third sentence would be: "Her home is up for sale at a loss and her French antiques are at the flea market - sale priced to sell "as is." When I visit Pat, there is no noise, no clutter, no football helmets nor basketballs on the kitchen table. For over 10 years, I searched for something unclean in that house. One day, I hit the jackpot! I found her porcelain coffee pot filled with stains. I immediately poured bleach and water into the pot left a huge note with instructions on cleaning that type of coffee maker. That coffee pot saved our friendship!

Sue at least has the grace to admit that housework gets her down. She has three wild boys like mine so there's no need in her lying to me anyway. But I can finish a phone conversation with her in which she has remarked that her house is a mess and I can dash down the street with the hope that her home may look as wrecked as mine. I walk in to see gleaming tables, windows shining, no fingerprints on the woodwork and beds made with no lumps. She also painted part of the house and wallpapered the entrance hall and bathroom. Anyone with three young children who can wallpaper rooms, paint the panel in the family room, keep up with the washing and still smile should at least get a letter of praise from the President.

Sue's event that saved our friendship occurred after her son's long illness and surgery. I made a casserole for them the day they came home from the hospital. At 8 PM that evening, the phone rang. The voice on the other end said, "Can you eat Saran wrap?" I answered, "Sue are you crazy?" In desperation she said, "Don't argue with me, just look at the ingredients on the box and see if it can be eaten." When I finally got the whole story, I learned that she had left the wrap on my casserole and baked it. I loved her for that. She had redeemed herself with me.

Our Dogs Have Character

With this new, awful disease called Parvo spreading in our community, I was reminded of all the traumas we have had in the past with our dogs in spite of our efforts to give them good medical treatment. Then my thoughts wandered to all the dogs we adopted over the years from the animal shelters in other towns before we moved here.

Most people have such good luck finding brilliant pets at their local animal shelter and it is definitely the best route to take as the pets there are truly orphans. However, we seem to have had a series of bad luck with every dog we adopted at a shelter.

Lest someone criticized me about that statement, I go on record as saying that an animal shelter is one of the most worthwhile projects any town can have. Being an animal lover myself, I strongly support these facilities. It was just our misfortune to select – over a period of years – the only retarded dogs in the place.

Our first "find" was a black and white spotted puppy that was intended as a pet for our "then" only child. That dog cared about only one thing – food – and lots of it. The dog didn't love us, the child or anything else in the world except food. I first attributed his hunger to his "lean days" but that was no excuse 10 months later. We had to give him away when he attacked our small son as the child walked by the dog's food bowl. (That crazy dog was convinced that our son wanted the dog food.)

The next dog was a cute, black puppy that was going to be a very small dog – so the lady told me. That dog, in three months, grew to the height of my waist (and was still growing) and had a spiteful attitude toward life and people. I got rid of that one (to a good home) by throwing our uncooked dinner – raw steaks – into the car of the dog's new owner just to get the animal in the car. It was definitely worth it! That was, however, years ago when beef was cheaper.

My husband accused me of selecting such dumb dogs that I sent him to pick out the next one. That last adopted dog from the shelter was a sad situation. She was a smart dog. I'll admit that. But she was also sick. In fact, she needed a full time doctor and nurse in attendance. The few dollars it cost to adopt her were pennies compared to the cost of bringing her back to health again.

The first week we had her we spent three visits with the vet. He informed us of her delicate health and started treatment which will eventually cost about the same amount if a family member had a major operation. That same weekend, the dog suffered a setback. We were unable to reach her own vet so we rushed her to an animal emergency service. (That was the first time I ever heard of such a place but if you own enough pets, you'll learn a lot.)

When we called to report the dog's relapse to our regular vet, he told us to bring her in immediately. He checked her over and prescribed more medication. He also handed me a book (as thick as a small dictionary) which contained a place for the dog's picture and detailed facts about our dog's strange medical history, her treatment and a record of her current shots. The vet informed me that I must keep the dogs record with the at all times and bring it for each checkup to keep the records updated. (At this stage in my life, I had had numerous dogs, was the mother of three children but had never experienced anything like this.)

It was then that I just went over the edge and lost my mind. I looked that vet straight in the eye and told him that I had no idea when my children needed their shots, I had no handy medical records on them and I certainly didn't plan to haul around dog records complete with picture when I had no immunization records on my own children. From that day on, the vet disliked me because I wasn't serious enough and he preferred my husband to bring the dog and in because my husband was more polite and respectful.

Much later, after we had moved here, the same dog was hit by a car and spent long periods of time in our new vet's hospital. She never fully recovered and we lost her after months of treatment and anguish. But to the vets here who tried to save her, I commend them. Never have I seen people work so hard for so long to save an animal.

So the only dog we ever got at the shelter who wasn't crazy did, eventually, cost us a small fortune starting the first day we adopted her. But I think we would do it all over again if we were faced with the same problem.

Our Son's In College

Several times in recent columns, I have mentioned the heartbreak of the son or daughter graduating from high school and going away to college – from the parent's point of view. It is well known that most parents do suffer emotionally when their children leave home. Naturally, I assume that the beloved child would feel some of the same emotions. That shows you how much I know about kids.

I should have suspected the worst when we went to look over the college with our son for "Parent's Weekend." While all the parents were discussing the courses and meeting the instructors, our son and his friends were gazing off into space. I wrongly assumed that they were realizing for the first time that this would be their home, were having misgivings plus second thoughts. I then saw that the space where they were gazing was filled with some very pretty freshman to be girls.

While the parents were taking a walking tour of the campus, the sons were darting back and forth from their soon to be dorm to the swimming pool. I later learned that they were checking the distance from their dorm to the swimming pool (filled with girls sunbathing) to see if field glasses would be needed.

Being a parent, I thought, "Well, they will certainly feel differently when they really get to school and learn that we are no longer close by."

Our son has been gone a considerable time now and we have not received that first letter although my husband and I have worn out the door on the mailbox opening it and closing it. The only time he has called has been prearranged by us. We call him but he doesn't reciprocate.

The first few days were awful for us. At every meal, we would look at each other and wonder what he was eating and where. He then told us he had found some great places with "specials" – all you can eat for four dollars. (After feeding him for a few months, the restaurants will be bankrupt and he may miss home then.)

He did write my aunt and told her he liked school and was not at all lonesome. I asked her to let us know when she heard from him again.

I guess this all goes to show how much we really know our own children after living with them all these years. I wonder if our college son even remembers our address.

Please Pay Mothers by the Hour

We've all heard jokes about possessive mothers, unfair mothers-in-law and mothers who never think that the mate of her son or daughter deserves her child. Well, upon reflection, it's no wonder some mothers feel that way. Think of all the time, tears, money and part of "herself" that each mother invested in raising her children.

Can you count the hours you have sat with and cared for your sick children? Can you count the hours you lost just waiting up for them to come home at night? What about their problems, worries, victories and defeats? Didn't you take each problem and situation personally? What about those wrinkles under your eyes and those gray hairs – mixed in with your natural color? Every gray hair in a mother's head has a child's name on it.

While you were raising your children, you gave them their vitamins, straighten their teeth, repaired their wounds, watched them cross streets safely, drove them miles and miles for years to all their activities, helped them with their homework, talked to their teachers, mended their clothes and their egos. There's no way in the world to count those hours and those years when you were "on duty" 24 hours a day.

Do you think that your son-in-law or daughter-in-law is going to invest the same amount of time with your child? The answer is "No!" The reason is that you have already raised that child who is now an adult. Actually, when your child marries, you are simply handing over the finished product to his or her mate.

It's no wonder a mother is reluctant to give up her children just when she (with Dad's help too, of course) has brought them to a point when they can converse well, display good manners, don't mumble, be respectful to older people, eat correctly at the table and are generally ready to face the world.

Raising children and then having them marry is rather like training a team for the Olympics. Just at the moment of glory when they have won the Gold Metal, the team runs off for parts unknown – never to be seen or heard from again.

Raising children is also like raising a world champion walking horse. You (the mother and trainer) toil, train and work every day. You hope for the best. When the horse wins the championship, there are numerous people ready with offers. Then comes the big offer that is too good to turn down. The horse is sold and the trainer is left with an empty stable. The new owner, who didn't put one ounce of work into training that horse, can now just bask in the glory of ownership.

In spite of the trials, the tears, the concerns and the years of work, most mothers will tell you – as I do – that in the final analysis, it was well worth it and we would do it all over again – if given the chance!

Recalling Summer Vacations

In a recent column, I described an eventful (and dreadful) canoe trip during one of our vacations. There is yet another summer vacation that I recall with misgivings.

This one was a trip to the beach just after our youngest son had seen the movie "Jaws." Although I enjoyed the movie, I knew it was a mistake to let my son see that film just before our trip.

This happened years ago (before "Jaws II and Jaws III") and my son was a very young child. He assured me that he knew it was only a movie, that the shark was not real and that he was old enough to handle that movie.

Well, like all the rest of the audience, we all screamed during the chilling scenes, held our feet up under us in the seat and waited helplessly until Jaws was finally killed. That first night after the movie, my son slept with his brothers, refused to take a bath and later would not go swimming. We finally coaxed him to the swimming pool but the second he thought darkness was near, he would leap out of the pool and disappear.

Then came the trip to the beach. He refused to go past the sand castle (a fortress he had built). Everyone in the family did their part in trying to help him overcome his fear but to no avail. The awful part came when he started warning other tourists. He would sit on the sand and shout praises like "Danger, shark infested waters!", "Sharks nearby!", "Careful, beware of sharks!"

This went on and on. Once we carried him into the surf and he clung to us like he was on a lifeboat in the middle of the ocean. The poor child was convinced that with every breaking wave there was a giant shark coming his way.

You can imagine our fun at the beach with a terrified child screaming "Sharks, Sharks" all day. The stares and rude remarks from other tourists didn't add to our enjoyment nor help to ease our guilt over letting him see that movie. He definitely was the delight of the local Chamber of Commerce. It's a miracle that we were not asked to leave immediately.

Now he has grown older and even made it through "Jaws II". It's time to go to the beach again and "Jaws III" is being advertised. (Will that shark and his descendants haunt me forever?) My son just informed me that he wanted to see "Jaws III." His older brother laughed and said to him, "Just when you thought it was safe to go back in the water" I can't win!!

Recovery Time

For some parents September is considered "recuperation month," a time to rest up after having the children home all summer. In my case, I said goodbye to our house painter and sent him back to high school.

Our teenage son, the house painter, entered into an agreement with my husband for painting the exterior and interior of our home. The exterior was to be painted first. I tried to reason with both parties about this not working out but no one ever listens to me. I did, however, state that when the time came for the painting of the inside, I would move out. (I then secretly checked the weekly local motel rates.) They both laughed at me and shook hands on the deal.

The first week was torture. The heat was unbearable and I could not turn on the air conditioner because the upstairs windows were open and being painted. Slowly, all day, every day, I heard shouts of requests like, "Mom, bring me some water;" "Please throw up the flyswatter and the bug spray;" "I need more ice in my glass, its melting fast in this heat;" "What's for lunch today?"

The radio then entered the scene. I heard blaring music all over the neighborhood and went outside to see what was happening on our street. Instead, I found my son on a ladder painting to the popular tunes and completely oblivious to the fact that he was creating a public noise nuisance. I ran upstairs and found the radio on my dresser connected to a very long extension cord and playing so loudly that I rushed to turn the volume down. In my haste, I fell over the cord and knocked the radio off the dresser. I was blistered with comments about breaking the painter's brother's radio which our son had borrowed without permission from our older son. It was my fault, of course.

By that time, I was seriously considering the motel for the entire summer. But a glimmer of hope came when he said that he would finish the painting job in record time. Ha!

After the first week, I was deaf anyway so I wandered around the house fighting off a heat stroke, fixing lunches, hauling cold water to windows, falling over paint buckets and washing out paint brushes which were found in the kitchen sink and crying softly to myself.

Now came the visits. All the painter's friends dropped by to see how he was coming along. He would come down off the ladder and chat. He called that his "breaks." You know the dialogue, "I need a break every few hours, Mom." When he wasn't visiting, I was answering his telephone and taking his messages. Some were more urgent which required him to come down and take the call itself. This was usually when he discussed his plans for the evening. The un-urgent ones were written down and passed on to him during his frequent "breaks."

By the end of the second week, I was incoherent and the painter was planning to paint only in the mornings and take the afternoons off. After all, his social life could not suffer completely!

His father objected when he learned how much time our painter was taking off but I reminded him that they had made the deal and suggested that he talk to our painter. Besides, I didn't have time. I had my hands full answering phones, taking messages, fixing lunches and snacks, taking water and cold drinks to windows, falling over extension cords and destroying radios. There is only a limited time in any day and my days were full.

My patience snapped after three weeks when I had run up and down the stairs twice in five minutes and was then told that the cup of water I had taken to the painter didn't have enough ice and the cup was not clean. I lost my cool completely! When I gave him my comments on the situation, I was as loud as his radio.

Now the painter and his father are discussing fees and I only want to be there so I can submit my own bill – for combat pay!!

Saying Goodbye To My Washing Machine

It is hard to say goodbye to an old friend but I think I am seeing the demise of my washing machine.

Every housewife knows how important, how respected, how necessary a washing machine is to the well-being of the lady of the house. A friend who is a mother of four children once confided that she needed her washing machine more than she needed her husband. (He was away from home often but her washing machine stayed right there in his place all the time.) I would never make that statement but I can certainly empathize with her,

I am experiencing the same emotions about losing my washing machine as I felt years ago when the family bid farewell to the diaper man. With two small children in diapers at the same time, that man was a welcome sight every week. Even he got misty eyed when he made his last trip.

Now, it is almost parting time with my washing machine which has served me well and faithfully for years. That machine has had many homes, seen the arrival of two children and numerous pets. The only fault I found with it was that it had nervous attacks and stop working over holiday weekends but then, nothing is perfect.

This machine has had more parts than the Bionic Man. It has endured my anger when it buzzed from overload. It has tolerated all kinds of soap powder and liquid detergents. It has absorbed the shock of a college student throwing four huge trash bags of dirty clothes int the utility room and knowing full well that It would have to wash all those clothes in record time, It has taken all sorts of abuse from chewing gum to copper pennies for years.

When I think about it, that machine got very little praise for all its efforts. Not one of us in the family ever said a cheerful word to it. Perhaps if we had been kinder and praised it occasionally, it would have lasted a few more years.

I guess this proves the old adage that you never appreciate something until it's gone.

Simplicity of Children

I was watching some kids play in the swimming pool the other day and was amazed at what little it takes to make them happy. It was good to see how inventive they were.

A group of boys found some paper cups, rolled them into balls and had a water baseball game. Who, but children, would have thought of making paper baseballs out of used paper cups?

I remembered a Christmas many years ago when we noticed how quiet the house had become. We assumed the boys were playing with their new toys and were surprised to find that they were playing instead with the empty, discarded gift boxes. My father commented that perhaps that was the Lord's way of keeping children happy - especially those whose families cannot afford a big Christmas.

How often do you see a child's room filled with toys and find the child playing with pots, pans and spoons from the kitchen? Some children are even more interested in the ribbon from a package than with the gift inside.

Look at all the fathers who buy their sons elaborate electric train sets when the child is really too young to enjoy such a gift. These fathers have a great time running those trains while the small son sits by and watches.

Mothers do the same thing. They often select sophisticated dolls with elaborate wardrobes, admire their selection while their young daughters find their favorite old dolls and enjoy them as if they were new.

Many times, I have purchased complicated gifts for our children which were impossible for us to understand. One such item was a popular, fast selling game. That game came with four pages of instructions in small print which would take a week to read and even longer to understand.

I've seen young children receive expensive, fine tents when they really liked a blanket thrown over a card table better.

As we grow up, it is said that we lose the imagination of small children. The wrapping, ribbon and box no longer hold a special joy. We adults just hurray to look inside for the larger gift. At that point, we have lost something priceless that children possess all through their youth - imagination and the joy of simplicity.

Snowbound With Children

The confinement during this past cold winter has driven me to make a few comments about being snowbound with children:

1. To enjoy the snow, it is not necessary to change clothes four times a day. Either stay inside or go out long enough to enjoy the freezing weather. Make it a lengthy stay outside and everyone should come in at one time. Stragglers who appear every 15 minutes are not appreciated.

2. The human body will survive without 6 cups of hot chocolate in two hours.

3. Yes, I know the snow is lovely but nevertheless, I still decline the invitation to sled down suicide hill.

4. When the summer clothes were packed away and winter ones replaced them, I put out all the gloves and hats in their proper places. Since no one living in this house moved them, I can only assume that they walked off by themselves. It is not my fault that a pair of boots and mates to three pairs of gloves have vanished.

5. Just because winter boots don't fit doesn't mean that you cannot enjoy the snow. Plastic bags secured with rubber bands will keep feet dry for a considerable time although I know it is not fashionable.

6. Bicycles, roller skates and skateboards are not the safest items to use on ice although it may be exciting to try.

7. If you do not get along well with a friend for long periods of time, never invite that same friend over to spend the night when a blizzard is predicted.

8. There are some mothers who do not enjoy having ice and snow thrown at them. It is wise to learn that.

9. Cars have to travel on ice and snow and the "roller derby crowd" should always give the right-of-way to the driver.

10. If you have been ill and out of school for several days and make a miraculous recovery on a snow day, it is still

advisable to wait 24 hours before you go out and enjoy the great outdoors.

11. Snowbound mothers with children at home tend to become nervous after the first day. It is advisable to consider the mother's feelings. Remember when the ice thaws those same mothers are quite capable of driving off into the night – never to return.

Spray Can Irritation

I've heard that the man who invented aerosol spray made a fast fortune. If that's true, I hope he keeps armed guards around his home. If the housewives of America ever catch him, he will wish he had never thought of an aerosol spray.

I'll be the first to admit that it was a good invention but it was never perfected. How many times have you started cleaning the oven and have the spray can fail when you are half through it?

Nothing makes me feel as stupid and helpless as staring at ½ full bottle of spray cologne and not knowing how to get it out of the bottle. I have stuck pins in the valve, hit the bottle on the sink and even tore off the top and tried to pour cologne out. None of those tactics work by the way.

Then there is the spray insect repellent. The spray usually lasts to cover your arms and the rest of you is fair game for mosquitoes. The same is true with spray spot removers. You'd better aim the spray for the worst spot because it will never last to cover all the soiled area.

Notice the messages on these cans and bottles. "WARNING: Avoid contact with food. Avoid direct spraying into eyes. FLAMMABLE: contents under pressure. Do not puncture or incinerate container. Exposure to temperature above 130°F may cause bursting." In other words, the cans will burst, blow up and burn!

I was meeting a friend for lunch the other day and she was very late. When she finally arrived, I noticed she had a most unusual fragrance. I asked what cologne she was wearing and she looked me straight in the eye and said, "Flower Garden." "I've never heard of that," I said. She laughed and said, "I guess not. I just made it up." She explained that she started with a rose fragrance cologne but the spray failed. Then she switched to lilac and the same thing happened. She finished with Lily of the Valley. "The combination is very unusual. Why don't you wear that all the time?" I asked. "Are you kidding?" She said. "The sprays on all three bottles of cologne are forever stuck. I can't get another drop of cologne out of those bottles."

Spring Can Be Depressing

Warm weather is causing the "fatty's" to slim down for the summer months ahead. As much as I love spring, there is a depressing moment when I think of my swimsuit image. Many people feel the same way, which accounts for the tremendous sales of diet books.

I have just finished a diet which lasted 11 days (or was it 11 years?) The diet was actually planned for 14 days but I arranged a trip, went out of town and cheated for the last three days. I certainly learned things about dieting, people and the psychology of dieting which I think are worth relating.

First, dieting ruins your social life. (But being chubby doesn't help it either.)

Secondly, if you have been an on and off again dieter as I have for years, your willpower isn't as strong as it should be.

Your friends encourage you to diet but then they stop inviting you out for lunch. Who wants to dine with a haggard, hungry, miserable looking person who can have only a teaspoon of cottage cheese and a lettuce leaf? Who wants to eat with a person who begrudges every bite her non-dieter friend takes and run the risk of having the non-diet lunch snatched away and devoured by the dieting friend?

A third fact that I learned is that some of those little sugar-free mints can have as many as 50 calories each. That was a shock because I was eating them with gusto to take the taste away of artificial sweetener which I used in everything from iced tea to salad dressings.

The fourth fact concerns dieting with a partner (which is suggested for moral support.) That is not all that it's cracked up to be. In my case, my husband and I went on the diet together. He lost over 10 pounds and I lost five.

We starved together but he was more successful. (Maybe it was the sugar-free mints I ate all week.) Can you imagine the resentment and jealousy the slow loser feels when she sees a smiling face of her partner after he has weighed in and announced his shed another 2 pounds?

The fifth thing I learned – and the most of important – is that dieters sometimes suffer from temporary insanity. Take the example of our diet director (my aunt.) She was on the diet with us and was dedicated to our mutual effort. However, we learned early on the diet that she was cheating on the side.

On one trip to the grocery, she grabbed three bags of chips and started eating them all right there on the spot. When our son reminded her of her diet and remarked that she, as our director, was setting a bad example for us, she screamed, "I bought these chips and I intend to eat them all," and she threatened his life if he squealed on her. That was a clear case of temporary insanity.

Standing Appointment at the ER

Any family with three or more boys should make a standing appointment at the hospital emergency room (ER), keep a handy supply of Maalox, tranquilizers and pray a lot.

For years, I was a standing joke in my former neighborhood because of my weekly trips to the hospital with one of the boys. The doctor in the ER was a personal friend of ours and advised me "To begin using a sand filled sock if I was going to continue to beat the children because it doesn't leave much of a mark." When I moved, a former neighbor wrote to say how much she missed seeing my car roar by with the latest accident victim. That's the kind of comments I can live without.

There is always one child in every family who is a daredevil. (That's the child with the old gray-haired mother.) In our family, it's the middle child. In one week, he broke some kind of record for accidents. He was barely learning to walk when he fell off the top shelf of our floor to ceiling bookcase, had stitches, removed same stitches, bumped into a door knob which blacken his eye and ate a part of the deodorizer in the toilet bowl. I knew that one of us would never live long at this rate. I really suspected that I would be the first fatality since he always had the first emergency treatment.

At age 5, he decided that he could fly. His first attempt was made from the top of my antique couch which resulted in my best table lamp being broken. He was Peter Pan that day and I literally wished he had flown to Never-Never Land. Then we had to replace the neighbor's storm door because he jumped through it (He was Batman then.) I have never understood how he managed that without a scratch (perhaps by then his little body was toughened by so many previous stitches.) In any case, he was so proud of himself that he re-enacted the scene with the neighbor's son taking a picture of him.

At age 8, he had moved to bigger and better things. We had just moved to another town when a large German shepherd attacked our tiny dog. The daredevil lost his temper and socked the beast in the face. (I wouldn't even go near the dog because of his size.) After other attacks on our car by the same dog, we decided to buy a can of dog repellent spray. The boys were lookouts but I was the only one authorized to use the spray. Then days went by and the dog was nowhere in sight. One afternoon, the three boys and I were running errands. I stopped at a store and left the daredevil and his other two brothers in the car. (The older brother was supposed to be in charge.) Just minutes after I entered the store, the youngest child made an entrance which would make a hailstorm sound like a summer rain. He was screaming, shrieking and crying so loudly that no one could understand him. I found my oldest son and the daredevil still in the car frantically reading the dog spray can ingredients searching for the antidote listing. The daredevil explained that he was demonstrating the correct way to use the spray and accidentally sprayed his brother in the face and mouth.

On the way to the ER. I ran every red light in town blowing my horn all the way. When we arrived, the ER doctor {by then my new best friend) calmed me and called the Poison Control Center. (The spray which I had bought had just come on the market so the doctor didn't have the antidote recorded.) As we left the ER, I heard the doctor say "Keep that number for the Poison Control Center handy."

Once again, we had established ourselves in a new neighborhood.

Summer Brings Garage Sale Mania

Summer seems to bring a sort of "garage sale mania." Those of us who love to plow through other people's junk really get into the swing of things when these sales start.

For years, I have dragged my family around to sales until they will no longer go with me. The only exception is one child who saves everything and considers every find a rare collector's item.

My husband says this mania of mine is a form of illness which affects people who secretly yearn to deal in junk. He also insists that I can "sniff out" a garage sale miles away before anyone spots a sign. His theory is based on the times that I located a sale in a deserted area of Kentucky Lake and on another occasion when I "sensed" a sale was in progress in a farmhouse which was 75 miles from civilization in Missouri.

During a sale, I walk around and browse for hours in the heat (or cold) digging in boxes of old books, trinkets and stacked up items marked, "Everything in This Corner Is 75 Cents." Yet my health never permits me to play golf in temperatures above 70° and if anyone suggests an evening walk in the summer, I say, "Are you kidding? In this heat?"

Recently, while visiting an out-of-town relative, the lady next door had a garage sale. I escaped on the pretext that I wanted to say "hello" to the neighbor. My husband smiled and told the boys, "Well, Mom will be gone for a long time because she saw that sale sign in the yard." So he took a nap.

Two hours later the boys shouted across the yard that we were ready to leave for home. I was frantically packing boxes of junk. When my husband saw all those boxes that had to be put in the car, he gave me one of those looks that husbands do so well and he was no longer smiling.

All the way home, I was told that I had to unpack my purchases immediately rather than leaving them in the boxes with other junk of the past. Then I was questioned where I would find room to put everything and what possessed me to buy all that litter (his name for my treasurers?) He even added, "I guess they sold out and closed their business when you left."

From atop a box somewhere in the car, one of the boys said, "Well, maybe Mom will be a junk dealer someday." "Someday?" My husband replied. "She already is a junk dealer and all that junk gets absorbed somewhere in the house, which brings up another point – don't you think the house is getting crowded and junky looking?"

I hear that same speech every summer. I think that going to garage sales is like gambling. Once you start it, it gets in your blood. I haven't met a man yet who has been able to break his wife of that habit if she is really addicted to garage sales. Probably the only cure is to lock her up or shoot her. If I'm not seen around town for a while, someone had better check on me!

Syrup Sopping in Loachapoka

Saturday, October 13th was an eventful and exciting day for me. I attended the Annual Syrup Sopping (for the first time) in Loachapoka, Alabama with my friend, Judy. Judging from the crowd and the traffic, it was a successful event. After recently having had a broken ankle, I may have been foolish to undertake this day but it was well worth the walking. The fragrance of the syrup, the barbecued chicken and the homemade biscuits was irresistible. I was reminded of my childhood days in Tennessee when my grandfather took me to a nearby farm to see how sorghum molasses was made. This syrup sopping event took me back in memory many, many years. Good memories flooded my mind. I was impressed with the friendliness of the people, the charm of the town and the talent which was displayed in the beautiful crafts. I even bought a decorative clip to wear in my hair.

Judy and I couldn't pass up the chance to have lunch so we bought barbecued chicken plates and then looked for a nice, shady spot to sit down. The perfect place "seemed" to be between two exhibits so we settled down to serious eating and then discovered we were sitting on top of an ant hill. A kind and generous exhibitor came to our rescue and one lady even loaned us her lawn chairs (while she stood with a child in her arms) so we could eat our lunch. A yellow jacket insect tried to share my chicken but I finally won after repeated attempts to chase him away by flailing my arms in the air. But these disturbances were minor compared to the fun of the day.

Our next stop was Slay's Apple Farm, North of Buffalo, Alabama, where I purchased some of the most delicious apples I have ever eaten. And the bonus was finding packages of soft, dry, fresh apple rinds which I haven't eaten since childhood.

Judy and I, being relentless shoppers, forged ahead to our last stop, The White Planes Country Fair. By that time, the crowd had thinned out to some degree and the heat of the sun had decreased and we were able to meet even more interesting people and see more beautiful crafts. There were 107 exhibitors there and I felt like I had entered an enchanted village at Christmas.

If I sound impressed, it's because I am. There is always something refreshing about exposure to beautiful handmade crafts and nice, friendly people. I came away from these events with a better understanding of Alabama and a sense of pride in the talent of the people here in this area.

Being my normal "ding bat" self, I did make one mistake. When I returned home, my middle son asked what I had clipped in my hair. I proudly removed the decorative clip and handed it to him. He started laughing and said, "Mom, this is a 'roach clip' used to hold marijuana cigarettes." I feel lucky not having been arrested.

Taking Care of the Aquarium

In another column ("The Oscar Fish Is Gone",) I discussed the recovery of parents whose children went back to school after this long, hot summer. In my case, I referred to our house painter (son) who returned to high school. Since some colleges start later than the high school, I have now said farewell to our oldest son who has returned to college and left us in charge of his aquarium.

Taking care of the aquarium would not be such a task if this son came home often to visit us and his fish but that is not the case. He returns home about three times during the school year and spends a maximum of 20 days at home during the summer.

He insisted on keeping these two large, ugly fish called Oscars who contribute absolutely nothing to the happiness and well-being of our household.

To fish lovers, the Oscar is an attractive fish and the larger ones are often more desired. But in my case, these Oscars show a definite antisocial behavior. Also in the aquarium, lives some sort of long, wiggly thing that is supposed to keep the tank clean. This servant fish must have quit his job the first week he came here to live. Now, he is fat, lazy and a freeloader who does nothing but swim around and hide when the two Oscars fight.

My son saw no conflict in keeping his aquarium here and returning to college 400 miles from home. He asked his brothers to care for his fish and got a tentative positive answer. The youngest son tried to feed the ones and was bitten. He quit his job. That left our middle son (the house painter) in charge. I will admit that he has proved steady and hard-working regarding this fish responsibility but other problems have arisen which further complicate a busy family.

The Oscars are so intimidating and threatening that no one wants to stay in that room. In the past, houseguests used that room when our son was not home. Now, no guest will enter there. We have an aunt who refuses to get near the tank because she is convinced that all three fish will leap out and attack her.

One fearless guest, who did stay overnight in the room, mentioned the noise from the aquarium, the fighting between the two Oscars, their frightening habit of lunging upward as if to escape and the fact that the bed is directly under the window which houses the aquarium. This guest used an electric blanket and feared all night that the fish would splash their way out in the water, would send her into electric shock, not to mention emotional shock, at seeing those fish jump onto the bed.

I have already made a statement that if perchance the fish do escape from the aquarium, they will stay where they land. I am a compassionate woman but there is no way I will rescue those ugly, ill-tempered Oscars and their companion.

Okay, so I don't get "Humanitarian of the Year" award. It's worth the sacrifice!

Teach Me What?

How many of you husbands have taught your wife to drive, play golf, tennis or bridge? Next question: If you answered "yes" to the above question, are you still married? The longer I am married, the more convinced I am that a husband cannot teach his wife anything. He's too emotionally involved to be patient, impartial or polite.

Fortunately, I was a licensed driver when I married (although my husband questions that fact.) He still will not let me drive on a trip unless he is totally exhausted. Then he takes a three minute nap and swears that he's refreshed, rested and ready to take the wheel again. Actually, I'm a good driver but no one can keep their sanity when the front seat passenger is shouting instructions and predicting a head on collision momentarily.

I think he lost confidence in my driving two years ago. We were on a trip and he was taking his three minute nap. I was trying to merge into a busy interstate in a heavy rain. I have the windshield wipers on low when he opened his eyes and screamed "Turn those windshield wipers on high!" He startled me so that I hit the wrong button and the wipers stopped completely. I stopped the car and a big truck behind me slammed on his brakes and veered off the road. You can imagine the conversation the rest of the trip.

After that, I refused any help or instructions from him, but recently he decided that he wanted to teach me to play golf. I had a sense of impending doom before we started. The first ball that I hit was supposed to go straight but went completely to the right and almost hit him. After that, he yelled "fore" and dropped to the ground every time I started to swing. That didn't exactly instill confidence in my ability. Before each swing, he would recite the same thing, "Keep your head down, eyes on the ball, left arm straight, and knees bent." It was awful. I just chopped up the golf course and the ball stayed in the same place. Finally, he was so disgusted that he ran up behind me, whacked me behind the knees with a club while reminding me to keep my knees bent. I folded up and sprawled on the ground. That whack was supposed to be instructional but I have since learned that in football, it is called "clipping" and carries a penalty.

If I ever play golf with him again, I will insist on a football referee being present.

Teenagers Give Hope

Who says that most teenagers today are no good? Who tells you that most of them smoke pot, drink excessively, are immoral and irresponsible? I hear this often and in some cases it is true. In some cases, it is true about adults also but few people make that generalization. It is true that today there are many temptations which confront the young people but that doesn't mean that they all fall prey to it.

In my opinion, today's teenagers are better informed, more serious, more patriotic and more concerned than any group of young people to grow up in years. I don't remember the tenderness, the interest and the readiness in my teenage peer group that I see today in this young generation.

Children today, from an early age, know what is happening in the world and most of them care. Because of the news media, education, parental discussion around the dinner table and the closeness of worldwide communication, youngsters see, hear, think and form opinions.

Take the event of the former American hostages in Iran for example. What child do you know who was not aware in some way of that situation? (And I found that teenagers had very strong opinions on this subject.) This was especially evident to me on the afternoon of the hostages release when they were airborne and on their way to freedom. It was late afternoon and I was walking down the aisle of a bookstore when I heard a very small child talking seriously to his mother. He said, "The hostages are free. Our people are free now." I looked down into the face of a little boy who couldn't have been over six years old – and I suspect even younger.

How many young men have you heard who are willing and ready to protect this country? How many have said, "Someone has to do it." How many did you hear express a willingness, even a desire, to take part in an effort to free the hostages when they were still in Iran? I have heard many and I know they meant what they said. They were so outraged that our – their – countrymen were taken prisoner in a foreign land that they were ready to help out. It was not just idle talk. It was the talk of young men and women who sincerely believed that they had a responsibility to protect our freedom and our people.

As a mother of sons, the last thing I want is a war. As a citizen and a human being, the last thing I want is a war. So I'm not waving the flag or working for the recruiting office through this column. I am simply stating a fact that we have good, decent teenagers today. When I hear people talk of the many teenage vices and "rotten kids," I wonder who these people will call upon if (and God forbid that it should happen) when time comes for someone to defend us and our right to criticize.

As a mother, I realize that teenagers are not perfect. The same is true of adults and they have had a longer time in which to perfect themselves.

It is time, I think, to find the good in those young people who deserve it. It is time to help put some good into those who need it. It is time to listen to what they have to say. They may surprise you. You may just want to ask, "When did they grow up?" "Where was I when it happened?"

Thanksgiving Poem

Adults tend to forget that wisdom and vision came from the very young. I was reminded of that fact on Thanksgiving by a poem written (for a school assignment) by my son, Jimmy, 13.

I would like to deviate somewhat in this column from humor to a subject more serious and touchy – being thankful. I want to share with you a special blessing – this poem – which spells "THANKSGIVING."

Thank God for all of your blessings.
Have turkey with a lot of dressing.
Always be thankful for all of your food.
Never on Thanksgiving be in a tacky mood.
Kiss your mother so she'll be glad.
Shake the hand of your dad.
Give your friends a great big smile.
Insure that love will last a while.
Very good chefs should be asked to cook.
Insure that they follow the book.
Nice people are very rare.
Give your family a hug and show them that you care.

By James R. Bowman

The American Family Is Breaking Up

We are always being told that the American family is breaking up. Marriage is going out of style. Couples are deciding not to have children.

In some cases, this is true but for the majority, marriage and parenthood are thriving. The home is the essence of our country and I expect to see it stand as long as we have mothers and loved ones who care for our children.

I don't mean babysitters or housekeepers or indifferent people who are paid to tend to our children. I mean people like mothers who have an abiding love, and unselfishness, a desire to make a happy home for the little people who are entrusted to our care.

Motherhood is far more than just having a baby. It takes courage, time, pain, tears, smiles, a sense of humor, patience, luck and faith to raise a child.

Today, I am dedicating this column to mothers in honor of Mother's Day on May 13.

She's the one who thought you were beautiful when you were born. Many people said, "What an ugly baby." She remembers every person who made that remark and sends your most flattering picture to them each Christmas.

She's the one who stays up with you all night when you are sick and still smiles at you the next day.

She takes you to the doctor and waits hours for the doctor to diagnose what she said you had last night.

She's the one who counts the gifts under the Christmas tree to be sure that you get your share.

She's the one who shouts at you, "Put on your hat and zip up your coat," when you get out of the car at school. You want her to self-destruct because all your friends are looking at you but she hangs in there protecting your health.

She's the one who tells you a million times to clean up your room. She threatens to call the Health Department and have both you and your room condemned. But she has the grace not to laugh when you joined the "Don't Litter, Keep America Beautiful Club."

She's the one who never hears what you tell her, forgets everything, is absent-minded to the point that you consider trading her. But strangely she remembers the hour you were born, all the shots you need before entering school and camp; and she remembers to wash your clothes and cook your meals, take you to school and attend all your school programs.

She's the one who waits for you during music lessons, dancing lessons, football, baseball and basketball practice. She is seen most often sitting behind the wheel of a car. She's the only person in the world who has learned how to read a book, write a letter, plan her meals for the next week, make up the grocery lists, sleep, mend, plan a party, balance her checkbook and have her weekly nervous breakdown – in a car.

She's the one who has to borrow money from you all the time. But if the chips were down and you are in need, you'd get her last dollar.

She's the one who occasionally (and unfairly) compares you to your brother or sister. Her only defense is that she is trying to make you improved, to strive for higher and better goals. The comparison is her home spun psychology – her way of saying, "You can do just as well, maybe better. Try!"

When she's moody or cross and snaps at you, forgive her. She's a human being trying to fulfill a role that was meant for saint. The human part of her betrays her at times so show some compassion.

When you come in late at night, she's the one who is awake waiting for you. She may be pretending sleep but she's really waiting for your footsteps - the signal that all is well.

She's the one who has saved every card and gift you ever gave her. All your crayon drawings, hand painted flower pots, your first baby shoes. All these treasures are carefully packed away but kept by Mother for later years.

When a relative or friend makes an unkind or unfair remark about you, she's the one who will have a few words with the offender. Her few words could fill a dictionary. She will never forget the offense. Forgive, perhaps. Forget, never.

You are the only person who can hurt her, embarrass her, disappointed her and still get another chance at her friendship and love.

No matter how old you become, you won't escape Mother's advice, her concern, her affection and her presence in your life. The day all that ceases, she will be gone forever and you will wish you had her back.

The Canoe Trip

Spring vacation means a week away from school and plans for family trips for some of us.

One of our boys suggested that we go to a state park for fishing, horseback riding, golf and some trips down the river in a canoe. They all talked about how much fun we had on our last canoe trip. It's funny how each person sees things in a different light. I remember that canoe trip as a disaster!

On that first trip, we were transported to the river in a little van with no door. We drove through woods and on a road that only a tank should have attempted. That ride to the river was enough to cause heart failure in a well person.

The driver – our guide (as he called himself) – drove at break neck speed over that awful road and across a bridge that should have been condemned in 1937.

Throughout the ride, the passengers were being thrown back and forth while enduring dust which blew in the van and covered us completely. I couldn't open my mouth to shout for help because of the dust so I clung to the seat which rocked back-and-forth as I was hurled about. The boys loved it.

I was convinced we would never reach the river alive but when we did, I was a shattered, dusty wreck. We had some friends with us and one of them couldn't swim. She would have left instantly if she hadn't felt that the canoe trip on the river was safer then taking that van back.

Our "guide" was to meet us at a certain spot down the river so we set off like Indians in three canoes. Our non-swimmer friend was so petrified that she wouldn't move an inch nor speak for 15 minutes.

Actually, I enjoyed the trip even when we turned over numerous times. The water wasn't very deep but those rocks sure were sharp. Two and one-half hours later we reached our destination but the guide was not there. (From the beginning I knew he was the type to run out on us.)

I was sorely tempted to let his canoes float on down the river but the rest of the party overruled me. We were selecting one adult and two children to run miles to find our trusty guide when finally, we heard a loud, bumping, rattling noise and saw our "Jungle Jim of the River" speeding down the road in his van like he was competing in the Indy 500. I then decided to walk back even if it took two weeks until my husband assured me that the trip back was shorter and not on the same road.

I couldn't believe it when my family thanked the guide profusely for the wonderful trip and even took his business cards if ever we were back again.

The boys recently asked for the guide's card because they wanted another fun filled day on the river. How can I tell them that I tore up those cards and threw them away the minute I reached the lodge last year?

The Car Pool

Much has been said about carpools. They are a blessing and a curse. A carpool is somewhat like a teenager – difficult to manage but you wouldn't dream of giving it up.

There are many mothers who detest carpools. I, at one time, was in that group. With only one child, there is no reason for joining such an organized group. If you plan to stay healthy, never have car trouble, no emergencies must ever arise and you enjoy driving all day.

I am convinced that women who can organize a carpool, keep it running efficiently and manage to keep her passengers and their mothers happy can, indeed, run the government and handle the most tedious and difficult negotiations. I really don't understand why politicians haven't yet recognized that fact. If I ever hear of a woman running for office who is a mother and carpool member in good standing, she will get my vote. That's a woman who can handle any job.

Children are so busy today that mothers carpool everywhere. The standard approach is, "If you drive one way, I'll drive the other."

Many years ago, I knew a woman who was so hung up on carpooling that I expected her to organize the entire neighborhood. She literally invaded my life. She should have been running the Marine Corps.

She would call and issue brisk, rapid instructions: "You are to drive on Tuesday and Friday this week – both ways and Monday and Wednesday next week. Pick up the younger children first then on to the junior high. Never leave a passenger but if he or she is late, demand an explanation and apology."

"We can't let tardiness get out of hand and set a bad example. If the children are noisy or rowdy, stop the car and take their names. Turn the names of the offenders over to me and I shall contact their parents."

I lasted three weeks in her carpool. My children were rowdy. My children were late. My children were never in the correct "pickup place."

She kicked us out of her organization and I've never been so relieved. She made it plain; however, that our expulsion was similar to being released from the Army with a dishonorable discharge.

The funniest story I know about carpools involved a lifelong friend of mine. She has four children in four different schools and runs in all directions at all time. She called one day just before the start of school and asked, "Bitsy, Am I correct about this fact? I think I have four children or do I have five?" Incredulous, I laughed and said, "Of course you have four. Do you want me to tell you their names?" "No," she said, "I'm just checking. I've had many phone calls to join school carpools and I have joined most of them. Now, I am in five carpools to five different schools - one of which none of my children attends."

Well, I know how she feels. I have days like that.

The Children's Transformation

Just before approaching the teenage years, a strange transformation comes over children. They become vague, restless, unsettled and seem to be drifting away from you. They also fall into one of two categories: 1. The "I'm Right and Know It All" type and 2. "The Mumbler" type.

The first category is usually an extroverted, outgoing person by nature. (Although shy, quiet children have been known to get into this group at teenage time.) This "I'm Right and Know It All" type will argue with you with the skill of an expert trial lawyer. He will break down your defenses, wear you out, endure so long that you are ready to give in to anything he suggests. (And he does this cheerfully and with a smile.) He knows all the answers. Parents begin to think it is a miracle that they have survived so many years without the sage advice and counsel of this teenage child. Whenever there is a disagreement, this teenager is never wrong – all the other family members are to blame. This type has to have the last word. Exhaustion of the person having a different opinion has been a winning tactic for him. He will never give up. His opponent either hits him our surrenders. Since this type is the nucleus of activity, the "live wire" of the group, every phone call is of the utmost importance. The President's "hotline" isn't as vital as the phone is to this child.

"The Mumbler", on the other hand, only communicates with a select group: his friends, the stereo, the car, the TV and the credit card. This type wants to be a rich orphan. Hand over some cash, no questions asked. You are concerned because "The Mumbler" is not talkative until you observe him in a group with his own friends. Suddenly, "The Mumbler" changes, blooms and really has fun. Then you realize that he just doesn't enjoy your company. I call this the anti-family stage.

161

A typical conversation with "The Mumbler" is as follows: **Parent:** Where are you going? **Mumbler:** Out, **Parent:** Out where? **Mumbler:** Oh, just to goof around. **Parent:** And then? **Mumble**r: Then what? **Parent:** Will you be home early after goofing around? **Mumbler:** No, I'll probably go to a party. **Parent:** Where? **Mumbler:** Not sure yet. Party may be called off. **Parent:** Who is having the party? **Mumbler:** Jack, somebody. Forgot the last name. **Parent:** Well, where is it? **Mumbler:** Not too far from here. **Parent:** How will you find the place? **Mumbler:** I'll see the cars. (Which explains part of the energy crisis. They drive all over town looking for a house with a lot of cars.)

Never under any circumstances, mix the two types of teenagers in one household. The only thing they share in common is the love of the telephone. Mixing these two groups can be catastrophic.

If you do have a "I'm Right And Know It All" type and "A Mumbler" type in your home, follow these survival directions: leave town quietly at night, leave no forwarding address, have your mail sent to General Delivery in another state, send cards only on holidays (with no return address), pray, rest and reestablish contact with your children when they are grown.

The Decaying Me

I am by nature an impressionable person. I relate so totally to suggestions that I cannot watch medical television programs or read medical fiction stories. The last time I saw a medical program was, I think, Dr. Kildare. (You know how long ago that was.) By the last 15 minutes of the program, I had listed all the symptoms of the patient on a piece of paper; I had the exact symptoms and pains to match and it took days to convince me that I might, with luck, make it a few years longer. So this will show you how terrified I am of hospitals, doctors and nurses. These people are my friends out of their white coats and uniforms. This is the only area in my personality where I am a complete and total coward. I always admit it at the first when I am meeting someone professionally in the medical field.

About my 37th year, I noticed that I was like an old car; I needed new parts, repair and a tune-up. In three years (age 40), I would be known as that "40 year old fall apart." I had heard of this in the past but had laughed and said it would never happen to me, but within one year, I had consulted doctors-specialists for the following:

1. Arthritis
2. Teenage acne at 38 (During teenage my complexion was flawless.)
3. Bifocals (The doctor laughingly told me to come back when I couldn't read the newspaper. I had protested that I was too young for bifocals. He knew I couldn't read the paper when I came in.)
4. Nerves
5. Stomach – Colin trouble (A direct result of too much highly seasoned food and too highly seasoned 3 sons.)
6. High blood pressure (which started in my mid-30s. It was not helped when my little toddler ate 1/3rd of my prescription 5

163

minutes after I arrived home from the doctor and pharmacy. That resulted in a worsened condition for me and a 3 way emergency call to my doctor, the baby's doctor and the hospital.

7. Orthopedic shoes (That was the final insult. Actually, that's why and when I took up golf. I passed my shoes off as golf shoes.)

8. Hormone therapy (The Great American Novel should be written about this.)

9. The dentist

The dentist was the worst recent medical experience for this cowardly patient. Although in the past, I have had extensive and expensive dental work. (My dentist took an extended trip to Europe and sent me a postcard thanking me for the trip while I set home with a mouthful of gold crowns.) My last checkup was not as dreaded by me as usual. I wrongly assumed that 1. What else could go wrong as everything was new and replaced and 2. As you age, you have less cavities. That was my mistake. I should have been frightened in advance and prepared myself for what was to come.

The dentist had a new assistant who was to clean and check my teeth - all routine. He had just sent her to a seminar. That was his mistake. This young lady greeted me and put me in the sleek, modern dental chair that felt like a recliner. Just as I was starting to relax, she plopped a black tape recorder on my chest. That shocked me but she explained that the recorder was to tape her conversation as she checked my teeth for cavities or possible problems. (I didn't understand that "possible problems" bit.) She started talking to her tape recorder using long, complicated medical terms - not one word of which I understood. I became anxious and started breathing heavily (and possibly fouled up her recorder.) I was still waiting for her to simply clean my teeth.

She lowered her eyes and gave me a grave look. In sad tones, she said, "You have a disease!" I panicked and said "A disease? What disease? I just had a checkup 6 months ago." "You have PD Disease," she said and she made it sound fatal. "What in the world is PD disease?" I asked. Then I pulled myself together and said, "Now look here young lady, I'm older than you are and I tell you that you have to be careful when you tell a person they have a disease. That's just not how you do it. I am nervous. I've had a lot of medical problems lately. I have high blood pressure and I've never heard of PD disease." "It's Periodontal Disease and I'll have to take immediate x-rays to determine the damage," she answered gravely. Then I was escorted into x-ray. I asked for a magazine – something light and funny like MAD. She handed me a brochure. On the 1st page in bold, huge, black letters it said "You have PD disease."

With that, I just blew my cool and became completely hysterical. I started screaming for the dentist and in my anxiety even called him by the wrong name. He rushed in. I know the screaming and crying of a 40 year old patient wasn't good for his business. He quieted me, rushed his assistant into another room and closed the door. Then a few minutes later, he suggested that I go home and come back in a few days for a cleaning.

After he left, the assistant rushed out and told me I couldn't leave until she had made an appointment for me with a PD specialist. I literally grabbed my purse and ran out of the office.

A week later, the dentist had his secretary call to schedule another appointment for me and to inform me that he now had a new assistant. After they promised me she was gone, I went back.

I learned that every patient she had seen (since her seminar) had been told they had PD disease. It was a comfort to know that huge, grown stable men had fled that office in terror of her. I was not a coward alone. Somewhere out there, more cowards are hiding.

The Family Dog

Almost every mother gets talked into accepting a family dog. If she is lucky, she may get one who is toilet trained and obedient (all the things her children were not.) If a mother is new to this experience, she will accept it with a smile and a challenge. If she has had prior experience, she will write a contract and require the children to sign it. If she's really smart, she will convince them that the contract is legal and binding. A breach of the contract is punishable by no desserts, no vacations, no allowances and no car. If worst comes to worst (which it usually does in the case of a new puppy), she can assign double duty to all the children to watch the dog day and night.

We have had a variety of dogs - most of them retarded and one who was supposed to be a toy size but grew larger than my 6-year-old.

This last puppy was my downfall because he decided to love me as much as the children. (A mother is definitely defeated in this case.) If I am gone for an hour, he greets me as if I have just returned from the Grand Tour of Europe. (My children never show that much interest.)

We did have a little problem housebreaking him. I spent ages outside so he would learn what grass is used for. Finally, we developed a system: Immediately after his meal, I would yell "Take MacArthur outside! The child on the duty roster for the day would grab the dog and run outside like an Olympic sprinter.

When that problem was solved, MacArthur developed another bad habit. He had a fondness for chewing toys and furniture. So far, he has destroyed Superman's head, Batman's leg, Robin's hands and part of the Incredible Hulk. Then he moved on to bigger things. He tore all the fabric from the sofa cushions and pulled the foam and stuffing out of the couch. Next, he started chewing on the edge of the carpet.

Just before a trip to visit my aunt, I asked my husband to talk to the boys about their behavior. "I'll talk to the boys," he said, "But you talk to that dog! Tell MacArthur that he is one step away from the dog pound if he continues to tear up everything we have." Then he said, "By the way, why don't you take the dog with you?" Sadly I admitted, "He wasn't invited. The last time we were there, he ate Aunt Punk's draperies."

The Family Neurotic

Every family has a neurotic. Ours was Cousin May. I was really fond of Cousin May but I was never able to have any illness which was more serious than hers. In fact, she must be a walking, talking, living (barely, according to her) phenomena. She actually had the same ailment (but more severe) then the person discussing the illness with her.

When I became pregnant, my husband grinned wryly and said, "Call Cousin May and see if she can top that." (She was 65 then.) She did! I had to listen for 45 minutes about her serious and complicated pregnancies.

She has had four major operations, foot and bladder trouble, nervous condition, gone through the "change of life" for 35 years, the "heartbreak of psoriasis" (twice), constipation and diarrhea, sinus, allergy and eye problems, whiplash, falls and fever blisters.

If I were 500 miles away and had a virus that was "going around", it would have already reached Cousin May. Sometimes I have suspected that she catches things through the telephone.

She will use your prescriptions and share hers. When you are with her, it's like attending and American Medical Association convention.

One day, I decided to divert her mind from her illnesses and give her a problem to solve. I thought it would be good to try the shock treatment on her and let her dwell on someone else's problems for a while. So I called Cousin May and said, "Sam is leaving me after 15 years and 3 children. He's running off with his secretary." Cousin May sighed and said, "That's terrible dear. I never felt too sure about that boy. Have you heard that I'm having terrible problems with my hemorrhoids and may have to have surgery?"

The Feeding of Many

We often hear the expression "enough food to feed an army." Did you ever think about how much food it takes to feed a high school football team? The facts are staggering.

I recently helped, along with other volunteers, to prepare lunch for the high school football team before school started. Believe me, I'll never complain again about having to cook for a family of 5. My hat goes off to the manager of the cafeteria and all the others who make one meal possible for the kids at school.

Our day started at 8 AM although the manager, Charlotte, was there before we arrived. We walked into a spotless kitchen which made mine at home seem ready for a condemned notice. The first thing that caught my eye were the huge sinks. They were so large that you could be lost in one for a week if you had the misfortune to fall in. The cooking pans were gigantic and held 100 servings in each one.

That day the menu was hamburgers, French fried potatoes, tossed salad, baked beans, iced tea and cookies. I thought, "I can handle that. No problem since I fixed it a million times at home." Before I could tie my apron, Charlotte had given us all our individual assignments, pulled out numerous huge pans along with 12 very large and heavy cans of beans, 24 packages of buns, 50 pounds of ground beef, 8 heads of lettuce, 4 bags of radishes, 3 large cucumbers, 2 bags of carrots and a sack full of tomatoes. Everyone worked until 11 AM and then got ready to serve.

I was beginning to think we were entertaining the Red Chinese Army for lunch. At 11:30 sharp, the hungry team came in and the line was endless. When the steam from the warming pads finally drifted away, I saw that the food was gone. Everything was eaten. I couldn't believe my eyes.

The kitchen was cleaned and returned to its original state. My curiosity made me ask Charlotte how much food we had cooked. She casually answered "79 pounds of beans, 60 pounds of French fries, 192 buns, over 195 hamburger patties, four huge bottles of assorted salad dressing, 10 gallons of iced tea." "And", I added with a laugh, "cookies that were on a tray large enough to use as a sled this winter."

"Charlotte, how in the world do you feed them like this every day?" I asked. She smiled and said, "Oh, today was a slow day. We only fed 75. When school is in progress, we feed 700 every day for lunch." If that day was "slow", I hope she doesn't need me for a busy one!

The Fourth of July

This week we will be celebrating the Fourth of July. I want to relate a story to you which exemplifies the reverence and honor for our flag which a group of Girl Scouts from Kalamazoo, Michigan displayed as an example to all of us as Americans.

This flag team of scouts was made up of 3 Brownie Scouts, 3 Intermediates and 2 Cadets ranging in age from 8 to 14. Their leader, Mary Lou Erlenbush, was a respected, strict and dedicated leader having trained as a scout under the leadership of her mother, Mrs. Ethel Hart (my next door neighbor who told me this story.)

Mrs. Hart's training was instilled in her from previous leaders (who also trained as scouts and in later years became leaders themselves) as far back as 1919.

Mary Lou Erlenbush had taught her flag team the correct way to handle the American flag. Her group often was asked to perform because of its discipline, dedication and excellent training.

To be eligible for a flag team, each girl had to have perfect inspections: clean hands, hair, uniforms, socks, shined shoes, white gloves, all badges and pins on including the red flag team sash. It was considered an honor to be a member.

At one affair, this flag team started the procedure to enter a room by taking the standard two steps and waiting before it entered. When the girls saw to their horror that no one was standing, the Brownies shouted, "We stand when our American flag is presented." It was later reported that a multitude of feet hit the floor at one time as everyone present stood when the flag passed by.

Later the Kiwanis Club of Kalamazoo was having its annual dinner and one of the banks was presenting them with an American flag, they asked Mary Lou's team to do the flag ceremony.

The team arrived with 3 flags cased – Brownie, Girl Scout and American. They put their cased to flags in the corner and when the time came to use (uncased) them the president of the bank started to help. One of the little Brownies looked at his hands and then politely informed him that he could not touch the flag because he was not wearing white gloves.

After the affair was over and the flags were being taken to the car, the man again offered his help but explained that although he didn't have white gloves, he had found a pair of clean gloves which he could wear while handling the flag. The little Brownie looked him over and reluctantly said, "Well, I guess it will be okay now."

Needless to say, the bank president, the Kiwanis and all the people who heard this story have never forgotten it. This episode proves that there is still a special feeling for our country in the hearts of many Americans It is real patriotism when a small child stands up to an adult and teaches him (or her) the proper way to respect our flag. Often you sense this same feeling when citizens stand at attention, salute our flag or place their hand over their heart when the national anthem is being played.

On this July 4th, let us reflect on the real meaning of the occasion and dedicate ourselves to uniting this country. It is my wish that God will continue to truly bless America and it is my constant prayer that we will live in peace.

The Free Gerbil

A friend suggested that I write a column about the "free" gerbil. I knew her gerbil story because our family was the follow on recipient of her extensive set of equipment for use by our "free" gerbil.

Her story begins when a generous friend who gave her children a gerbil at school. (I question the definition of "friend" in cases like this.) When the children came home with their new pet, the family went in search of gerbil lodgings. They were quite amazed to learn that gerbils live in gerbil houses (more like hotels with room service) which would make the best hotel look like a shanty. Gerbils live in swanky, high-rise, classy homes. Assembling those homes would make a genius go mad with frustration.

A pet shop gave the family the full treatment about housing, feeding and making a gerbil happy in his new surroundings. Exercise equipment was recommended to keep the gerbil fit and healthy. Items are available which induced the gerbil to get the proper amount of daily exercise. This included tubes to run through, a trapeze-like invention, cubes to wander in and out of and even a clear, round ball which the gerbil can enjoy when he takes an outing away from his home. He is placed in the clear ball and allowed to roll all over the house at will which usually causes panic and great distress to the lady of the house.

What my friend purchased for her gerbil complex included the following: a deluxe housing tray, top housing with wire mesh floor, telescope tube, pet house cover with latch, gnaw guards, chewables to keep a gerbil's gums and teeth healthy, vent discs and lift latch. Also included in her purchase were "add-ons" like activity houses and special containers for an afternoon nap.

After my friend purchased and assembled her items, you can imagine the exhaustion and expense involved, it was surprising that a few weeks later she was so happy to offer her complex to us along with her "free" gerbil.

We learned the meaning of the phrase "Beware of Friends Bearing Gifts (Sometimes.)"

The Goldfish Saga

We just had a calamity in our house. (We have them daily but that's not the point.) Abe and George died.

Abe and George (for Lincoln and Washington) were goldfish which my youngest son purchased in Nashville and brought home the following day. He had called long distance to tell me about them (as if I would be ecstatic – which I was not) and I suggested that he name Abe, Robert E. Lee instead. Offended, he said, "I like Abe Lincoln and that's his name."

Well, Abe died the morning after his arrival. When I broke the sad news, my son said, "Mama never did liked Abe" – as if the fish was a family pet who had resided in our house for years.

That same evening George died. More tears followed.

I wasn't allowed to give them the usual goldfish funeral – flushing them down the commode while humming taps. No, the children insisted that Abe and George were to go out with full military honors.

I found a small, white box on which I wrote Abe in large letters. Later, I added the name George in equally large letters. The fish were wrapped in transparent paper and padded with cotton. (I thought that was rather generous of me since I wasn't attached to them and was even accused of disliking Abe.)

Two days went by and they were not buried. All those elaborate funeral plans were forgotten. Finally we said, "Now boys, you have till sundown to bury Abe and George or we will dispose of them in the usual way."

It was then that they reported they have lost the bodies. A search was started and finally the fish were found, still in the white box, under two old telephone books, a magazine and a calendar in the back corner of the kitchen desk. (That certainly shows you how much the boys loved them and wanted to give them a big sendoff, doesn't it?)

But true to their word (late but true), they invited several neighbor friends and dogs and the funeral possession marched from the backyard to the woods where Abe and George were laid to rest.

Immediately after the funeral, the boys went back to their play. It's certainly remarkable how fast one can forget the departed.

The Laudromat Style

Some women always looks so neat and well turned out. No matter what they wear, they always look stylish and attractive. Then there's people like me who appear as if they have just rushed out of the laundromat and are wearing the clothes they just washed.

It's very frustrating to be in that last category. No matter how hard I try, I have a last-minute disaster and go out looking like the sinking Titanic. One Easter, many years ago, I proudly wore my new black suit and hat to church. I felt great that morning because I thought I looked well-dressed. When I came home and was hanging up the suit, there on the clothes rack was the skirt to my new black suit. (To this day I don't know how that happened.) I looked down at the skirt I had worn and discovered that it was an old, black one which didn't match the top – quite.

I recently went to a football game out of town and was told to dress for rain. I walked into the stadium wearing tennis shoes, my clear, plastic drizzle boots over them, a rain hat that looked like a large plastic flower with wilted pedals and there wasn't a drop of rain all night. See what I mean?

The same is true with my voice and image. I always wanted a deep, husky voice like Lauren Bacall. Instead, I got the type of voice that causes people to ask when I answer the phone, "Is your mother at home?" or "Dear, May I speak to the lady of the house?"

When I was a little girl, I wanted to grow up to be a mysterious lady. I wanted to be sleek, complicated and have people say, "You never know what she's thinking. She's so mysterious and exotic." Instead, people see me as a rushed, confused, disheveled woman who was always driving carpools and has three notes hanging in the car plus two stuck on my purse with tape. That definitely is not a mysterious image!

I was discussing this problem with a friend and she agreed that some women just naturally have style and class. I mentioned one woman whom I thought was just perfect looking and had all the physical qualities I would like to have. My friend said, "I agree, she is ravishing but didn't you know that she spends a fortune taking yearly trips to an exclusive reducing salon? She's also had a nose job and surgery to have her stomach "tucked." I could hardly believe it but it made my day. I always thought she was born that beautiful.

The Most Popular Song in America

A reader sent an article from the National Enquirer (by Tom Smith) which explains the story about the most popular song in America. Guess what it is? "Happy Birthday."

According to the article, the song, "Happy Birthday," is not a folk song which belongs to the public as most of us have thought. It was written in 1896 and the present version was copyrighted in 1935.

The song was written by the unmarried Hill sisters, Mildred, Patty and Jessica, who ran a private kindergarten with another sister, Mary, in Louisville, Kentucky.

The story goes that Mary came home one day and said she needed a new song for her pupils to sing the next morning. Sister Mildred, who was also a pianist and church organist, wrote the music while Patty wrote the original words which were: "Good morning to you, good morning to you, good morning dear teacher, good morning to you."

Some years later at a family birthday party, sister Jessica wrote the happy birthday stanza – the version we know today.

Would you believe that even that little song, "Happy Birthday," has caused legal problems? At one time, Western Union and the Postal Telegraph used "Happy Birthday" in singing telegrams but the companies had to switch to other birthday songs after the Hill sisters publisher, Summy – Birchard Company, demanded royalties. Every time the song is played or sung on radio, television and the movies, royalties have to be paid to the foundation set up by the heirs of the three sisters who actually wrote the song.

All these years, most of us have thought that "Happy Birthday" belonged to the public. But if you think about it, there's very little left today that is free – not even America's most popular song.

The Most Tedious Job

Would you be interested in knowing what is the most tedious, miserable and difficult job in the world? It is getting a first year college student off to school.

I really wonder why parents bother since it's a sad time having a son or daughter leave home and yet, if leave they must, then some organization and work must be done.

Actually, you are not just sending a person away, you are sending an entire room and part of the house along also. You run into little problems like learning that the school mattresses are not a standard size so those sheets have to be found. The windows are often not standard sizes so you hunt for a shade, curtains or something to cover the windows. You also note that neither of these problems seem important to the future student.

Then you look at all the junk in your child's room at home and know it is impossible to fit all these "necessities" into the room at college. If you are smart, you will say, "It can't be done so grab what you want to take the most and forget the rest" but parents are not smart about these things and so have to persevere.

The next step is to enter the wreckage known as a teenager's room and try to find and organize the summer and fall clothes which will be worn at the start of school.

A fact which has been buried in your mind for years finally dawns upon you at this moment. Your child doesn't know what a closet is used for. Under the bed, in a corner, behind curtains, in a spare trunk – everywhere but in the closet. After all these years, you admit to yourself that with all the work you have invested is this kid, you didn't teach him about the uses of a closet.

The next job is to assemble all the clothes and see what fits. (This is done only by the bravest of parents.) Girls may be more conscious about their clothes. They often try to help but those of us with sons, all know how much a boy loves to try on clothes. They'd rather be thrown into a tank with Jaws.

At this point, you discover that 99% of the clothes do not fit and cannot be altered so there is a delightful chore of shopping for new ones. When the selections are made and a second mortgage is taken out on the house to pay for them, the battle is almost over.

You would be amazed at what boys do not think are important. (I hope girls are more sensible but since I don't have a daughter, I cannot speak for college-bound girls.) Unimportant items to boys are: curtains or shades, dress clothes, school supplies, medical records, pictures of the family, stationery and stamps to write home.

Very important items are: radios, stereos, posters, money, musical instruments, athletic equipment, mini-refrigerators and a supply of food to last through the winter.

When you mentioned towels, linen, a sport coat, tie and addresses of family members, they stare at you with a vague look in their eyes and mumble, "Well, throw that in if I have room for it."

I wonder if they realize they are going to college or do they possibly think they are taking an extended trip?

The Onion War

Have you heard about the war between the onions? (Yes, I said onions.) Through my southern heritage, I have learned about this war.

It all started in Vidalia (Southeast,) Georgia which is the only place in the world that produces the now famous Vidalia onion (famous for its sweet and mild flavor.)

In Vidalia, a place of pine trees and catfish, this onion is big business but the onion has caused many problems also. Arguments over what constitutes a true Vidalia onion has caused families and friends to feud, suspect each other of false certification of their onion crop and even caused one grower to slip into the fields with a borrowed sugar testing device to test another grower's onions.

True Vidalia onions are shipped within the United States and also to Europe. (And they are called "the caviar of onions.") They can be eaten like apples, are not supposed to cause indigestion (when ripe) nor even cause bad breath.

They are big in my hometown of Nashville, Tennessee and are selling for high prices. People eat Vidalia onion sandwiches as special treats. I have eaten one and must confess, it was delicious. The idea of a plain onion sandwich didn't sound appetizing to me but it lived up to its publicity in my opinion.

The war between the onions in Vidalia has caused rival onion festivals, cook-offs and even rival onion queens.

Because of the rivalry which had prevented the formation of a grower's association, counterfeiters have been able to sneak hot onions on the market labeled as Vidalia and threatened the Vidalia onion's reputation.

The true Vidalia onion itself is a fat, round, Texas developed hybrid named "Granex" that for some reason becomes better tasting, more succulent and sweet around Vidalia, Georgia. It is thought that the rainfall patterns and low soil sulfur content may bring out the best of this type of onion in the Georgia location.

For many years (before the onion became famous,) a supermarket concern sold the onion. They finally started putting all the onions grown in a 4 county area in southern Georgia into bags marked "Vidalia" and marketed them as the gourmet item. Then the trouble started. The Vidaia onion became a famous moneymaking item. With the moneymaking came the rivalry.

Onion growers from Glenville (approximately 30 miles from Vidalia) formed an association to monitor onion quality, had an onion festival and an onion queen. Vidalia, quite naturally, felt threatened because they had their own festival and onion queen. Vidalia started calling itself "The Onion City" (although the town's official slogan is still "The City of Progress.") The Vidalia Chamber of Commerce sponsored a character (in costume) known as "Yumion," a smiling, 7 foot tall onion who travels around Georgia as "ambassador" for Vidalia.

In an effort to set standards for the Vidalia onion, (to stop the imposters) growers from four counties around Vidalia organized the Vidalia Onion Growers Distributors Association. Other problems followed which caused some growers to withdraw. The situation had not been settled before last spring's harvest. However, most people involved did agree that with the depressed state of the farming economy of last spring, Vidalia, Georgia should not waste its biggest asset – the Vidalia onion.

The Oscar Fish is Gone

The Oscar fish who devastated our house is gone! Finally! It's an inside family joke that my husband declares that fish messed up our entire two-story house.

Reviewing my explanation written in a previous column ("Taking Care of the Aquarium",) the saga of the fish started two years ago when our oldest son set up an aquarium, added two Oscars and a fish to clean out the tank (who retired just after he moved in.) Then same son asked his two younger brothers to care for the fish as he promptly left for college only to return about four times a year. The youngest son was bitten by the large Oscar and immediately quit his job. That left all the responsibility on the middle son, Jim, and I must say, to his credit, that he did his best.

A follow on series of events the occurred – each one a crisis. The two Oscar fish grew to be huge and occasionally they fought each other. After a year, one of the large Oscars died. His death was followed by another death – that of the retired fish whose job it was to clean the tank. That left a huge Oscar by himself. The oldest son, Steve, lost all interest in Oscars and never even inquired about him. On rare visits, he didn't even bother to clean out the aquarium but Jim remained faithful to his duty.

One day we noticed that the remaining Oscar was failing in health. For several days we observed him. About the fourth day, Jim called me at work and said that he would have to go to school late because the Oscar was dying. Jim diagnosed that Oscar's tank was dirty and he wasn't getting enough oxygen. He suspected brain damage. (How does the fish get brain damage, I wondered?) For hours Jim worked and Oscar pulled through. Then the tank started leaking and my husband started shouting, "That fish is messing up the house." That was the chant we heard all the time. My husband decided to move Oscar to the garage. Jim protested saying the hot weather would kill the fish. The compromise was to move him to the family room. (My husband's master plan was to move him a little distance at a time until he eventually had Oscar out of the house completely.) All the time, we were advertising, "Large Oscar for sale: reasonable price." "Free Oscar to a good home." "Free Oscar to any home."

After the move to the family room, Oscar started doing peculiar tricks. He would swim to the corner of the tank and stare at my husband while he was sitting in his recliner. Oscar would stare for a very long time then he started swimming in a frenzy back and forth and would lunge upward throwing water on the wall and the carpet. My husband declared, "That fish is messing up the entire house."

After several weeks of this bizarre behavior, we all decided that Oscar had to go. A kindly person who owns a pet shop agreed to take Oscar on consignment. The day Oscar left our house was like watching "Wide World of Sports." My husband came into the family room with a fishnet that would have captured "Jaws." It was gigantic. Although Oscar was very large, he still had not approached "Moby Dick" in size. There was a fierce struggle as Jim and my husband transferred Oscar from the aquarium into a bucket. The result was water all over the carpet and the wall. Then they moved the new small fish (recently purchased) to clean out the tank into another bucket. To prevent Oscar from jumping out, they put a Frisbee over the bucket. Can you imagine the scene? They rushed Oscar to the pet shop and later told me that he was nearly unconscious from shock when they arrived. Then they dismantled the aquarium and cleaned the carpet and the walls.

At this writing, Oscar is waiting to be purchased. Do I miss him? You can guess the answer to that question!

The Peabody Hotel

The ducks have returned to the Peabody Hotel and I joined their parade!

Most Tennesseans know that the beautiful old Peabody Hotel in Memphis has been restored, redecorated and is now opened again. The famous Peabody Ducks which used to swim in the Peabody fountain/lobby pool are back again and still in the care of Mr. Edward D. Pembroke who is often called "Mr. Peabody."

Every day at 10 AM, Mr. Pembroke brings the ducks down to the lobby on the elevator from their roof top pool. As the door opens, music is heard and all the ducks walk in on a carpet and go directly into the fountain/lobby pool where they swim and stay all day. At 5 PM, the ducks get out of the water and stand on the edge of the fountain/lobby pool until Mr. Pembroke is ready to escort them to the elevator and back to their roof top pool for the night.

This is a dramatic event which is highlighted by a few members of the hotel staff standing at attention while the bell captain announces that the ducks are leaving for the day. The music starts and Mr. Pembroke signals for the ducks to walk down the few steps from the fountain/lobby pool onto the carpet and then they start their way to the elevator.

Guests of the hotel and tourists stand on each side of the walkway to watch and photograph the ducks. It is such a fanfare that one is reminded of the opening nights of a Hollywood movie in the past when movie stars got out of their cars and were mobbed and photograph by fans.

Recently, my husband and I stayed at the Peabody and I accidentally did a stupid thing which amused my husband. He insisted that I "tell on myself" in this column for a change so here goes the public confession.

We checked in about 4:45 PM and the lobby was extremely crowded. There was a long line of people checking in and I was restless waiting in line with my husband. I looked across the lobby and saw a gift shop. Shopping is my weakness, so without another thought, I said, "I'll meet you in the gift shop" and dashed off.

I did notice a lot of people around the fountain/lobby pool and a crowd forming a line on each side of the carpet to the elevator. Briefly, I wondered what these people were waiting for. I did not know the schedule of the ducks departure and really was not thinking about the ducks except to notice that they were charming so I said "Excuse me" about 20 times as I passed the fountain/lobby pool and walked on the carpet to cross the lobby. I noticed that people were looking at me in a strange way but my mind was on the gift shop. Then I heard music, saw cameras flashing and looked behind me and discovered the Peabody Ducks following me. Just as I reached the elevator, I sharply turned to the left and dashed into the gift shop.

My husband will never let me live this down! I lead the parade of the ducks and a friend said, I was "sort of like the Head Duck." I'm sure I spoiled many pictures, horrified the hotel staff and made many people wonder who in the world was crazy enough to march across the Peabody Hotel lobby in front of the renowned ducks. If I ever go again, I'll wear a disguise!

The School Project

Some time or another every parent has had to suffer through a school project. It is a painful experience.

There's the leaf collection, the term paper with footnotes, the science project and history project to name a few. Mothers and fathers run through fields and woods searching for leafs; they sit up all night helping with typing and spacing; they help research every historical hero and politician in the state and they dive in to assist in the science project which can become as involved as creating the atomic bomb.

All the time they are doing their work, for which they will never get a grade, parents state the age old complaint: "Why didn't you start on this earlier?" The answers we receive can be very creative like: "I thought I had two more weeks to complete this;" "All my notes are gone – lost, stolen or vanished – they have just disappeared;" "This teacher has no heart at all. She expects the impossible from us and never gives us enough time to finish anything" and "You remember I was sick last week and that is when I had planned to finish this."

There is absolutely no reason to argue with your student-child. Either you help him or you don't. It's as simple as that! No matter how you try to make your point about the pitfalls of starting late, your child will always out-talk you, out-reason you, out-argue you and exhaust you so just reconcile yourself to that fact of life.

When my youngest son graduated from the Cub Scouts, I foolishly thought the major projects were over. That shows you how smart I am! Last week he really dropped a bombshell on us. He has a 9 week project which is, of course, due before Christmas vacation. He planned to build a replica of the White House with sugar cubes. (When I heard this, I tried to check into the hospital but they did not have room for me.)

Yes, he has taken extensive notes, written a letter to the President and 3 more to our senators and congressman. Yes, he was sick for a week so that leaves us little time to get it all together. The world was not created in so short a time. When I told him it was impossible to build a miniature White House in that time, he looked astonished. He said, "You told me that very few things were impossible to do in life if you have the will and the desire." Now, the kid is throwing my lofty words of wisdom back in my face so here I sit - on the floor surrounded with sugar cubes while my son and husband try to put this White House together. Our house is a wreck, Christmas cards have not been addressed, Christmas shopping has not been done and even the evening meal has not been considered yet but here I sit working on the White House.

Merry Christmas and Happy Holidays to you. May there be no White House for you to build this December. That's the best wish I can give you at the moment,

The Sound of Christmas

December 25th was a Christmas of sounds this year. All day we heard crashes, explosions and noises like "beep-beep, dat-dat." This was the Christmas of electronic games, television games and puzzles.

I watched a little fellow with a mustache on a television game deal Black Jack over and over. When he won, he smiled and he frowned when he lost. He was more fantasizing to watch then the game itself. I heard space fights, auto races and crashes and saw little figures playing basketball on the television set while the players were being controlled by my sons.

After four hours of nothing but "quiet" noise from the family room, I checked in to see if everyone had fled the house and left the game still turned on the television. There I saw a sight I haven't seen for years. Two of my sons, who can't tolerate the presence of each other, set side-by-side happily playing a television game. It was the closest thing to a minor miracle and I bless the makers of these games. I can take a space war any day as long as it is waged on the television screen and not in the middle of the kitchen floor.

I'll admit that the next day the boys argued over little things like which game to play, who was taking too much time and one wanting to invite a friend over which would have eliminated the other brother from being a partner in the game. I expected that.

But for that one magic day, two brothers actually enjoyed each other. They laughed together, played together, set side-by-side for hours, didn't argue, no blows were exchanged and we had real peace in our house.

That may not seem like a big deal to some of you, but when you have lived through one Christmas after another of broken toys, cowboy guns that fire caps, toys that don't work, toys missing parts, fire engines with clanging bells, robots running under your feet, remote controlled cars that try to run you down, barking dogs who are frightened by the loud, moving toys, arguments over one toy given to three brothers and confusion all day long, you learn to appreciate the meaning of the word "quiet."

The little "beep-beep, dat-dat," crashes and explosions on the television games are mild in comparison. If children only knew it takes so little to make a parent happy.

The Sports Store

I am very un-athletic. When I was 8 years old, I had selected the names for my three future daughters. I always knew I would have girls. I envisioned my life having ribbons, ballet lessons, cheerleaders, beauty parlors, beautiful dance dresses, greeting my daughter's escorts at the door and waiting for them to come home and tell me all about the dance and the date.

Nothing prepared me for three boys but I'm a good sport and have entered into their activities with zeal. I drive (along with millions of other worn-out mothers) in the baseball, basketball, football and gymnastic carpools. The coach's word is law. At games, I am to be seen not heard. (That was a unanimous request from all three boys when I became too rowdy at a basketball game. No one will sit with me anyway.)

I have learned the code and the creed of the game. I'll obey it and live by it. (Never call the coach; never approached the field or court when your son lies unconscious and bleeding. Wait until after the game or until the ambulance is taking him away and then quietly and discreetly slip away to the hospital. Never cheer at the game. Never call your son by his name. If you get carried away and must express yourself, call your son by his number but never his name. Just yell "Way to go #31, great tackle #31" then hastily consult your program as if you are searching for #31's name.

After years and years of this, I still cannot handle one aspect of my life with the athletes. That's the sports store. The equipment is so foreign to me. Before my oldest son was driving, I outfitted him with the necessary items from the sports floor. But I always managed to embarrass him and myself. I am so insecure at the sports store that I now quietly drag my sons to the jockey straps or whatever looks necessary and whisper, "Do you need one of those? If so, get it and put it on the counter with the other things."

My complex started when my oldest son (then 8) needed a mouthpiece for football. This was my first child to enter sports and I wanted him to have everything that he needed. Before football, I never dreamed of things like his teeth getting knocked out. (At the first game, I was sitting very close to the field and heard the shoulder pads cracking. I thought it was bones breaking. A seasoned football mother administered ammonia to me.) I was determined that I would research the market and find out everything I could about a safe mouth piece and get him the best one available.

The man at the sports store knew what he was dealing with when I walked in. I had to ask where everything was and get his suggestions on sizes, weight, etc. for the pants, pads, and helmet. When I asked about mouth pieces, he showed me two kinds. One was a slip in. He said I didn't have to boil it but the fit would not be exact. Boil it? I didn't know what in the world he meant. I had boiled that kids baby bottles for a long time but I thought if he was old enough to play football, my boiling days for him were over.

Then the salesman showed me another mouth piece. He explained that the strap on it was to be attached to the helmet. That looked awful to me. I could see some brute ripping off my son's helmet and his teeth along with it.

Finally, I got the courage to ask about boiling. The weary salesman patiently explained that to get the correct fit, the wearer must first boil the mouthpiece for a few seconds, then put it in his mouth, clamp down on it while it is still soft and it would adjust to the size of his mouth. Then I did it. I blew my cover! I innocently said, "Well, now I understand but how in the world can he run somewhere a few minutes before every game and boil his mouthpiece?"

Never have I seen such an expression of pity on anyone's face. When that poor man explained that you boil it one time only, I wanted to die. I hastily bought three boilables and left. For two years, I would not enter that store. I would drive my son up to the door and wait in the car.

After two years, I decided to enter again. I reasoned that the salesman was probably not working there any longer or surely he had forgotten me. When I walked in the door, there was that same man and he started laughing as if I had come in just two days ago. After that, I traded out-of-town or by mail. When the boys were old enough, I gave them my charge card and drove off.

The Things Children Say

Through the years, I have remembered some amusing actions and dialogue from children – my own and others' – which I would like to share with you.

I've also heard some interesting definitions from children which, to me, sound better than the original names such as a "cross eyed puzzle" for a crossword puzzle and "handmade rolls" rather than homemade rolls.

Then there's always a child who refuses to eat a certain food at home and simply devours it somewhere else after the parents have said, "I'm sorry but he just won't even try that. In spite of our efforts, he won't take one bite of that vegetable."

It is especially embarrassing when the child asked for 2nd and 3rd helpings of the dish he "hates" and then eats the remainder from his parents plate. Parents usually want to sneak out of situations like that by dragging their child behind them on a path of rocks and nails.

When my brother was very young, he never had a large appetite. Mother cooked delicious large meals, especially for breakfast. One Sunday morning, I remember how my parents almost begged my brother to eat more breakfast before going to Sunday school. On that particular day, the Sunday school teacher asked every child in the class what they had eaten for breakfast. When she got around to my brother, he lowered his head and with downcast eyes he quietly answered, "I didn't have anything to eat except a piece of bread and water." My mother was so angry that she literally stuffed him with food all that day and sat at the table to make sure he ate everything before him.

I remember my husband spanking one of the boys and making him stay in his room. The child (then 3 years old) cried so long and so loudly that I finally went in to check on him. He looked at me and said, "I told you. I told you that Daddy was a dangerous man."

After our son had recovered from the chicken pox but still had a few spots on his stomach, we were in the middle of our airline flight to Nashville Tennessee. He stood up, pulled up his shirt and loudly announced to all the passengers. "Look, I have sugar pops on my stomach." The remainder of the flight was rather tense. All the passengers gave me dirty looks and were convinced that I had brought a contagious child on the plane.

Some years ago in Kansas, a little brother and sister who lived in our neighborhood came to all the nearby houses selling "paper." I bought a packet and later realized that they were selling their parents mail – bills, personal letters and everything that came to the house.

Recently, we were in a Nashville, Tennessee restaurant and I had a salad with bean sprouts on top. One of the boys looked in horror and asked what in the world is that stuff on your salad?" I said, "Surely you have seen bean sprouts before." After a moment's pause he seriously said, "Why didn't they let those little bean sprouts grow up to be beans?" How can I answer that?

The Word Is Hope

The New Year always signals a fresh start. For this New Year, I tried to think of one word which is important to dwell upon and I chose the word "Hope."

"Hope" is defined as: "To desire (something) with some confidence of fulfillment." (The American Heritage Dictionary.) Certainly, the word "Hope" is a powerful word. When you think about it, "Hope" is the one feeling we had that something makes us "hang on," "carry on" and keeps us going from day to day. Without "Hope", life would be dismal indeed.

Today, there are many things to hope for - some as a nation and some private hopes. As a nation, we can hope for peace. We can hope for the leaders of our country to have wisdom, compassion and knowledge to guide us through the times ahead. We can hope for better relationships between countries and we can hope for the strength to check those peoples and countries who ruthlessly advance upon weaker and smaller countries in their selfish desire to conquer. With this hope for strength, we need to hope that our leaders can use this strength to a peaceful advantage.

We can hope for a better economy for more jobs which will restore respect to those who want to work.

For our private hopes, we can hope for our children, hope for good health and hope for better family understanding and stronger friendships. We can hope for better education for our children and grandchildren and for good educators who will direct them in a decent path that stimulates their minds so that they will be ready to take over when our generation passes the responsibility to them. Each generation wants to leave a legacy for the next and each generation hopes to leave the world a better place than when they came.

Last but certainly not least, we can hope that those people who have no hope left within their hearts may find a cause to hope again. Happy New Year!!

Things Only A Father Can Do

A father is often the least appreciated person in the family. Everyone depends upon him but all too often we neglect to say "thank you."

I, too am guilty of forgetting to thank my husband for the important role he has played in my life and the lives of our three sons.

My own father deserves special praise for the love he has given me all these years. (Both men really deserve a metal for putting up with me.) This Sunday, I hope you will thank the man who has cared for you and your children – your husband, your father and everyone who has touched your life, your children's lives and left it better for his presence. So today, I dedicate this column to fathers everywhere in honor of Father's Day on Sunday.

A father is wisdom when tempers are flying and mother is too emotional to handle the situation. A father is taller and stronger than anyone else in the world when a child is looking up to him. God gave fathers the strength to stand firm and broad shoulders to lean on.

When an emergency arises, it is usually a father who can keep that's steel control while he is silently playing for everything to be all right. Everyone else is looking to him for comfort and strength. No one knows how frightened and insecure he feels because he doesn't show it.

Only a father can have the patience and enjoyment of teaching his little son to fish and play ball and to admire his daughter's new dress (even though he paid for it,) to check out her date in a polite way (while he prays that she will be safe) – and still enjoy being a father.

Only a father can smile with pride when his son passes down a pair of outgrown shoes to him. He feels the same pride when he is told that his daughter is smart as well as pretty.

Being a father is a 24 hour 7 days a week job with no vacations. Where- ever he is, across town, across state, across the world, a father is still in his child's heart and he feels the same. A father suffers, rejoices and grows with his children. As the years pass, a father watches his son grow and work toward achievements. When the awards are presented, a father stands tall with pride and has a special misty, wishful gleam in his eyes. He sees his son, an extension of himself, taking a faltering step toward adulthood. Although he knows he is losing a part of his little boy, he knows with joy that he is raising a man.

A father sees his little girl as a fragile, tiny thing who needs his constant protection. As the years go by, that delicate little flower starts to show a will of her own. Her father is baffled but amused. The day comes when her father realizes that his daughter is a woman. His pride in her is only diminished by the fact that she will leave – that someday he will have to hand her over to another man, her husband. But when that day arrives, her daddy will look at her through tear filled eyes and see a young woman ready to start her life. Then he will know that he hasn't lost her – will never lose her.

From little boys and girls to men and women, fathers have lived every moment. And so the process of life goes on.

Unusual Gifts

One of the most exciting aspects of Christmas is the unusual gifts we give and receive. I'm always looking for unique gifts and rejoice when I receive them. However, some people do not share my sense of humor and act horrified when they open a package from me which has taken considerable thought and legwork on my part to locate.

I'm like the elderly relative (on my husband side) who put a great deal of patience and time in the selection of her gifts to others. One Christmas she sent my husband a red and green tie with "Merry Christmas" written all over it with shiny, sparkling letters, and a blinking light in the center.

My gift from her was unusual, to say the least, since I've never figured out what it is (and that was 18 years ago.) She knitted me a long, woolen "something" about 12 feet long. I tried wrapping it around myself, then around the chair, then draped it over the couch and finally gave up.

Then there was the "space pipe" that I gave my husband one year. My rare find was black, silver and cone-shaped with a sliding screen to hold in the tobacco. When he opened it, I immediately shouted, "It's a pipe" because he looked so helpless and didn't know what to thank me for.

My brother laughed outrageously when my husband said, "Bitsy, you really do find unique gifts." Later my brother translated my husband's remark to, "Where in the world can she find such nutty things?" Unfortunately, the space pipe wasn't ready for the public. The sliding screen was too loose which resulted in burning tobacco falling out onto my husband's new slacks and burning a hole in them.

I was happy to find a kindred spirit who gave odd gifts at odd times when our 14 month old son received a cloth book (so he can learn to read early.) He really absorbed a lot of knowledge when he ate that book!

We don't mention the plastic monkey that I selected for our 2-year-old. I adored that monkey because it did jumps and flips. I could hardly wait for our son's delighted laughter when the monkey went into action. That child screamed for weeks until I finally had to give the monkey away because we thought the boy was getting a complex and would hate animals all his life.

Stuffed animals were another favorite on my list because I have loved them since childhood. One of my sons threatened me (at an early age of 10) by saying that he had tolerated teddy bears, a tiger so large that it needed its own room, stuffed mice with long yarn tails and numerous other creatures for the last time.

He made it plain that he would not appreciate a stuffed animal again for Christmas. That was the year I located the 6 foot shark (which took up all the space in the closet) and gave it to my middle. He was younger and showed more appreciation anyway.

The 5 foot inflatable clown for our 1-year-old was a disaster too. To demonstrate the clown's rocking ability, I punched it hard in the middle while the toddler was standing nearby. The clown fell on him and he cried all Christmas day. The clown departed the house soon after that incident.

No wonder I'm always late getting my shopping done for Christmas. It takes so long to find gifts that are really appreciated.

Well, I've Goofed Again

Well, I've goofed again! It's amazing how many stupid mistakes a mother can make without even trying. I was asked to reorder some checks for my son so I simply filled in the amount he wanted on his reorder form from the bank. It never occurred to me to check the "style" of checks as I assumed they would send what he had ordered in the past which was, I think, a style called "Hunting Scenes."

He was astonished when he received one hundred checks on which had pictures of an adorable, little rabbit. Naturally, it was I, (according to him) who made the mistake and not the bank. He informed me that he refused to carry the checks with little rabbits on them and he certainly would not cash a rabbit check. I explained that the bank had made a mistake and sent me the wrong color of my checks the last time I reordered but he still blamed me.

He even convinced his brothers that I personally selected those Bunny checks. They all said in unison, "That's just like Mom. She thought those checks were 'cute' so she ordered them." Then they went on to remind me of all the years I gave them stuffed animals until they revolted and of the "sissy" clothes I wanted them to wear. By that they met decent, clean, matching outfits.

They remembered when they went off to camp for the first time and I had put out matching shirts and shorts with clean, white socks. You can imagine my horror when they came in wearing red shorts, orange shirts and socks that had been mutilated from generations of washing and bleaching.

It was at that exact point in my life when I decided that their future wives would have to help them select their clothes. Obviously, they had no sense of color but would not listen to me so I said to myself, "Let them go through life wearing red and orange together. Just because I'm their mother doesn't make me responsible for their choice of clothes and the colors they put together."

Now, after the check incident, I find that I will no longer be in charge of ordering checks nor depositing and withdrawing money from their accounts. In short, I have been fired as their "financial aid." They think I am disappointed over this. Just wait until they have to do it all themselves then we will see who has the last laugh!

The next time any of my sons order checks, I hope all of them get a picture of a huge, brown Teddy Bear on the front!

What Is A Mother?

What is a mother? Mothers come in all sizes, shapes and colors. They don't necessarily have to give birth to a child – they can adopt one or raise one but all good mothers have some qualities in common.

A mother turns the other cheek more times than she can count. No matter how often she is hurt in some way by her child, a mother will not give up.

A mother gives of herself – her time, her energy, her mind, her efforts, her patience, her kindness, her ambition and her everlasting love.

A mother sacrifices – whenever there is a choice between herself and her child, the child comes first.

A mother suffers – the heaviest burden, the saddest heart, the fears, worries and grief over a child's problems are carried by a mother.

A good mother has no favorites but her "special" child is the one who needs her the most at a particular moment.

A mother remembers – she may forget today's grocery list but she can tell you in detail about her child's childhood even if that "child" is twenty or thirty years old.

A mother has a special smile that is unique to all others. That smile is visible when her child has excelled in some way or made her happy.

A mother is the most responsive person in the world to three little words from her child: "I love you."

A mother saves and collects – old cards, poems, pictures, handmade gifts, pressed flowers – everything which links her with her child.

A mother forgives – she may not forget but she is capable of forgiving her child faster and more often than she can ever forgive anyone else.

A mother accepts – whatever the child's shortcomings, a good mother accepts, goes on and continues to love.

From the very moment that a woman becomes a mother, she will be that – it is her role and her destiny – for the rest of her life.

May God bless each of you mothers who read this column and may your children honor you this Sunday in some way. Happy Mother's Day!

When College Causes Heartbreak

Last year I wrote a column about graduating high school seniors (my son was in that group) and the message was sad because my husband and I – along with many other parents – were experiencing the agonizing reality that our firstborn child was soon leaving home. Now, a year has passed and I have some reassuring news and hope. This column is for you parents who have just barely survived graduation and are sending your first child off to college in the fall.

First, you must realize that when your child does actually leave home for college you will again feel the same heartbreak that you felt at graduation. The first stage will last a week. That's the stage of shock. You will not be able to concentrate. With every bite of food you take, you will wonder if your child is eating even one meal a day. Your food will stick in your throat and every member of the family will pretend they are not hungry when they see that empty place at the table. These family meals will be strangely silent.

The next phase will be letter writing and sending packages. You will write at least every day (some mothers have been known to write several letters in one day. They are the extreme cases.) When you send the packages: cookies, candy, canned foods, peanuts and clothes, you will listen constantly for the telephone to ring.

At this point, I may add that your college child will probably not communicate with you too often so it is necessary that you establish a time each week for a collect call home. Your child (except in cases of extreme homesickness) is undergoing a great change. While you are suffering, your offspring is having the time of his (or her) life! Meeting new people and having all that freedom is exhilarating.

After 4 to 8 weeks, you actually accept the fact that your son or daughter is gone. You realize that life must go on and that there are far worse things than having a happy child away at college. Naturally, you never cease to miss them but finally you are able to handle it.

Finally, your child will come home for a weekend. You will cook and cook and have all his (or her) favorite foods. When he arrives, the family will be gathered together like a Norman Rockwell painting. This college student will come in and somehow look older, more mature and even taller. Everyone in the family will be asking questions and talking to him at once while he presents his mother with his dirty laundry – which has been washed only once in several weeks. You will be thrilled to wash all those clothes and linen.

The weekend passes all too quickly – with you washing, cooking, seeing your child occasionally as he runs in and out of the house, receives phone calls, visits and circulates around town. It is a wonderful weekend for you.

You never realize how much you enjoyed cooking and washing (honestly.) Then Sunday comes and your child gets into the car to go back to college. The family gathers in the driveway waving, crying softly and all the pain comes back. You start all over again – back to Phase 1, but this time it's not quite so bad or so long.

As the months go by, your college child finally realizes that college is not composed entirely of fun, freedom and parties (when the report card is sent home.) There are exams, homework, library research, papers to work on, washing and drying his own clothes, cleaning the room (maybe) and other responsibilities.

It is at that time that the parents smilingly hear, "Boy, Will I be glad to get home for a while. I like school and it would be great if I didn't have to study so hard, do all that washing, eat out so much. Suddenly, home looks good. Home looks bigger. His room at home seems much larger than he remembered it. The brothers or sisters constant arguing with each other doesn't seem so nerve-racking. Their bickering is now just "sounds of home."

Your college freshman can tell you how much it costs to raise a child from birth to age 21. He knows about detergents, stain removers and that clothes have to be separated in the wash due to fading. This is the same kid that had never noticed a washing machine before and never learned just where in the house it was located – then he left for college.

This is the person who suddenly thinks mom's cooking is super and tells his brothers, "Stop complaining about what mom has for dinner. Someday you will be grateful for it – after you are gone."

It all comes into place for the parents. Although their lives have changed forever, they know that home really is where the heart is and that distance and time have not snatched their child from them completely.

Where Are My Supplies?

Do you ever wonder what it would be like to live in a world where you can find sharpened pencils (or any pencil) in five seconds?

Why can I never find Scotch tape when I bought two new roles yesterday? I put the new tape in the kitchen drawer with three pairs of scissors. (I thought I had fooled the kids this time. No one will take all three pairs of scissors.)

When I started to wrap a birthday gift today, there were no scissors in the entire house. (The recipient of my gift will be the first person ever to have a gift wrapped in freezer paper with freezer tape and a note written with a pen that I use for chuck roasts, etc.)

When the price of stamps went up again, I rounded up all my old nine cent and thirteen cent stamps and bought enough two cent stamps to total fifteen cents on each letter. I methodically checked every stamp I could find to determine how many two cent stamps I would need. You guessed it, when I came home from the post office, all the nine and thirteen cent stamps were missing. Here I am with thirty-two cent stamps and no envelopes large enough to use them.

Everything I need in this house walks away. No one knows anything about the disappearance. I questioned everyone even the dog. At any given moment, I can find football helmets, old baseball trading cards, broken rubber bands, tennis shoes, an assortment of jackets and coats but never a pencil, tape or a pair of scissors. Even the glue has now joined the vanishing group.

I thought I had hit the jackpot when I found a tiny tube of glue one night. I hid the tube to use on the discarded stamps which some mystery member of the household had put on their letters, tore them off unused and tossed them in the desk drawer. (No one confessed to doing that either!)

When I started to use the old glue, I found it wouldn't stick then I discovered that it was glue for Styrofoam and glitter. I haven't had Styrofoam and glitter since I've made a Santa Claus out of an oatmeal box which was 17 years ago. (I suspect this is the same glue I used then and if my memory is correct, the glitter didn't stick that time either.) Once again, the kids have outsmarted me. They wouldn't dare use 17 year old glue. They just put it out to bate me.

This is the sort of thing that can drive a sane woman over the edge. Having wrapping paper and ribbon but no tape nor scissors is like having a new car filled with gas but no car keys.

No matter what the children say, I have made a nineteen year survey and concluded that a house without tape, scissors, glue and pencils is a house filled with children. Visit any grandmother, great aunt or family member without kids living on the premise and you will find everything you need to wrap a gift or write a letter.

Next year, I'm addressing all my Christmas cards and wrapping all my presents at an undisclosed place. I have a relative who has at least four new pins and six sharpened pencils on her desk. That's my idea of organization and luxury. I may move in with her if she will have me.

Where Does the Time Go?

We are close to beginning a new year and it seems that the old one has hardly just started. Every January, I remark how swiftly time passes especially as we become older. This year will, I hope, remind me to enjoy the people and things that are important in my life and to weed out the unimportant.

All of us live in such a hurried society that we often let life pass us by because we are too busy running here and there to notice the very objects that mean the most.

Our children and family make demands upon us and we hurry to fulfill them but as we rush through all the events in the lives of our children, we sometimes don't really enjoy them because we are tense and nervous thinking about what we have to do "tomorrow." Suddenly, our children are grown and we stand in awe and ask ourselves, "Is this possible? Only yesterday they were babies."

Upon reflection, we realize that the "yesterdays" turned into years and we were not aware of the time passing. We left a lot of questions from our children unanswered with the comment, "I'll explain that later." Later never came because we were too busy. We leave much advice unsaid thinking I'll talk to him about that tomorrow. Tomorrow is followed by many tomorrows and suddenly the time has run out, the child is grown and leaving home and we parents think to ourselves, "Why didn't I explain that to him? Why didn't I give her advice on that subject?"

Within large, rushed, busy families, attention doesn't always get dished out in equal proportions. Every family member has a special need and at times, one member may need more attention than others.

I cannot say that I have always given special attention to the one who needed it most at the time. I have tried but I'm sure that somewhere, somehow, I overlooked someone and then often the little problems of our children seem so small to us considering the larger picture. But how big a problem seems to a young person when he or she is facing a situation in which advice is needed. A short talk, a pat on the back, a smile can mean so much at times like that but often we are too hurried to take the time or, worse still, do not even notice the need.

I will always remember an incident which occurred years ago when one of my children told me that the teacher wanted some wildflowers from our yard to replant. We had lots of little, yellow wildflowers and I didn't mind sharing half of them with the teacher but I was busy, rushed and answered, "I don't have time to do that. Tell her I will send them later and I forgot.

It was sometime before I realized how much my child had dreaded to go back to school that next day without those little flowers and how hurt and embarrassed he was. Taking the flowers, answering a request, was very important to him and I let him down. Later, I apologized but the memory hurts me still and I cannot undo the damage nor take back the words. I won't have another chance. That moment has passed forever.

The same situation applies to friends who need us. Unfortunately, the world is filled with lonely, troubled, unhappy people. Sometimes if we but pause a moment, we can pick up the vibrations from a person who needs our friendship or help. I realize that we all are not social workers of the world but letting another person know we care means a great deal. A small kind effort can go a long way to ease someone's loneliness or trouble. Just being a friend and being there is important. True friendship and loyalty are rare qualities to be treasured for a lifetime.

In this coming year, I hope that all of us take the time to reflect on people and things that are important – children, family, friends and the way we spend our lives. We will never regret what we do in kindness but we will have a long time regretting what we do not do. In fact, we will have the rest of our lives to regret and remember.

If this coming year only brings me one thing: no regrets, then it will be a year spent wisely. May you also have no regrets and Happy New Year to all of you.

Whew – Those Last Few Weeks of School!

I don't know about all the students and teachers but the last few weeks of school nearly killed me and probably shattered other parents as well.

One of my sons had twenty-five reports to turn in, which I suspect, he put off until the last few weeks. There was a frantic rush to help him with the reports and with my little assistance, I learned more of Tennessee history than I ever learned when I went to school (about a hundred years ago.)

I discovered Tennessee governors, packs and treaties that I never heard of before. I met heroes, traitors and relived the founding of Tennessee and the Civil War.

Another son took on two projects that nearly wrecked what little peace there was in our house. First, he directed a movie about "Mr. Bill" appearing on the television program, "Saturday Night Live." His version of Mr. Bill's accidents were clever but the filming of a burning building (shoebox) in the backyard nearly finished me off. Then the movie film was delayed during processing and it had to be edited and spliced. I'm sure Cecil B. DeMille never had so many problems on his biggest movie.

Next came the leaf collection. All over town my son dashed pulling leaves off of trees. On a Sunday drive which was supposed to be a quiet, restful day, we found ourselves out in the country hunting leaves, stopping on the side of the roads, hanging over fences taking samples for his project.

When he had finished the leaf collection and put it in a binder, I thought his effort was worth publishing. I never learned all the proper names of the leaves but I sure became skillful at spying foliage and shouting, "Stop the car and get that leaf!"

Once again, I am glad to get out of school and start the summer. I guess the boys feel the same way. I've been too tired to ask them.

Why Do Teenage Boys Junk Up Their Cars?

It never ceases to amaze me how much electrical equipment and junk teenage boys put on and in their cars.

When I was a teenager and got my first car, I wouldn't have thought of "trashing it up" with all the things that boys like to add. (I did, however, consider briefly putting lacy curtains on the back windows.)

When our son got his new car, he polished and cleaned it constantly and vowed to keep it spotless. He even set rules for us when we were privileged to ride in it (which wasn't often.) He allowed no smoking in his car. We couldn't touch anything – not even the radio. We had to listen to "his kind of music" which was misery to me. We had to ask permission to open and close the windows and had to beg for the air conditioning to be turned on. He was saving gas and had to be one step away from a heatstroke before he would use the air conditioning.

All this madness lasted for several months and then he started to "add on" other items. He checked prices on cassettes and the cost of installation. He ran all over town comparing prices and finding "deals too good to be true."

Before we knew it, he was ready to add a cassette, remove the ashtray in the car for lack of room, add a P.A. system (so he could talk to his friends on the street while driving by,) add a power booster (I still don't know what that is) and finally, worst of all, add tailpipe extensions (which made that once lovely car looked like it was ready for the Indy 500.)

His dad spent an entire day (and a very hot day if that) on his head in that small car trying to rewire it. All the time he was working – upside down – he was telling our son that the tiny car did not need, nor should have, all that equipment in it. His advice was not taken, of course.

With the installation complete, our son went off happily with the P. A. system on, the cassette blaring a rock tune and the tailpipe extensions gleaming in the sun. Every time he drove off, I was afraid that car would blow up from an electrical overload.

When finally he did have trouble and the cassette and radio blew out, he was amazed that it had happened and dropped veiled hints that his dad may have not wired it properly. At that point, I washed my hands of the matter and told him of an old saying his uncle used, "Those who don't listen must feel." He didn't listen so now he had no music.

As he pondered his predicament, I was reminded of another old phrase which is so true, "The only difference in men and boys is the price of their toys."

Why Won't Men Drivers Ask Directions?

Have you ever noticed one of the basic differences between a woman driver and a man driver? Before you men say, "Yes, men are better drivers," I will tell you that this column does not deal with that subject. The real difference is that men will not ask directions and women will.

Over the years, I have done a sort of survey and always come up with the same conclusion. Women will stop anyplace every ten minutes to ask directions. In fact, I have formed some good friendships from being lost because I have met nice and interesting people along the way.

On the other hand, men are notorious for never asking for help. I'll be the first to admit that my husband was born with a good sense of direction and that same sense was left out of my head at birth. However, even he, occasionally gets lost but he won't admit it or stop to check.

I have seen a lot of country in different states while he drives around insisting that he knows exactly where he is going. I see this trait in our sons and I am told by many people (women) that their husbands and sons display the same characteristic.

There are times when it's frustrating knowing you are lost (especially when you're in a hurry) and yet the male driver won't ask for help. I have been known (to the everlasting embarrassment of my family) to shout from a window at a traffic light. "We are lost. How do we find...?" I don't get to finish my question as the light always changes to green and my husband peels off pretending he knows the way. I've considered writing in lipstick on the car door, "Help Us. We are lost." But if I tried that, I know my husband would push me out of the car and leave me alone to explain my actions.

Some time ago, my son wrote directions to our house for my father on an old paper plate. (My father lives in Tennessee.) Daddy carried that old plate for two years and finally lost it. The last time that he and mother came to visit, they were two hours late. They called when they came into town and daddy insisted he knew the way to our home. When they arrived, mother was furious! They had been driving around for hours and daddy had refused to ask directions. Mother said that she saw hunters in the countryside, the nice downtown, the shopping mall, the university and numerous schools. In fact, she would qualify as a guide for our town or the Welcome Wagon Lady, she said. Daddy's only defense was his comment that he knew they were close to our house so there was no need to stop and ask.

To men, admitting that they have lost their way must be connected with ego. To women, it doesn't seem that important. Perhaps women are just expected to lose their way since men enjoy telling stories about their wives who have no sense of direction. Everyone just assumes the poor woman was lucky to marry a man who can read a map and find his way. It's true to a point but it's also maddening to be the "dummy" in the family when you at least have the sense to ask for directions rather than driving through a large city four times – back and forth – insisting all the time that you know exactly where you are.

Winning or Losing With Grace

Much has been written about football and even more about athletics in general. I often wonder if we, as parents, get so involved in winning and having our children excel that we failed to emphasize two more important factor – sportsmanship and teamwork.

There's no doubt that we all want to win and no one ever wants to lose. No coach anywhere would be content with the team who showed good sportsmanship but constantly lost so I do not discount the importance of winning. Yet, when we, as parents and coaches, deal with young athletes, we hope that inside every boy or girl who participates in a sport there should be a feeling of winning or losing with grace and of playing hard for a team and not just for himself or herself.

I was reminded of this again when I read about the young Vanderbilt University football player, Marcus Williams, who played so well in one of their games that he was awarded a pair of black pants – a prize for Vandy players who performed up to SEC standards but young Williams declined the offer and explained, "As a team, we've come together….The closest this team has been in my 2 ½ years at Vanderbilt. We lose as a team and win as a team. I wouldn't feel right wearing black pants during practice this week. I didn't do anything special. Let's beat Memphis State and then the entire team can wear black pants." Of course, that game has long been over but the feeling of sportsmanship and being a team player still lingers on. Years ago, there was another team player who understood this message and he later became the President of the United States, Gerald Ford.

Sometimes the "nice guys" never earn the black pants but they stand on the side and support their team. There are many capacities for serving and some serve with no glory or praise by simply being there. How many years have you watched certain players' practice, endure all the rigors of training and yet they always stand on the side and never get in the game. They endure and go on. It makes one wonder why they are motivated that way.

I think that very few coaches appreciate this quality and even some parents fail to see it. We are so "hero" oriented that we only look at the "stars." Of course, no one person can be a team alone and it takes a very special sort of person to "hang in there" when he (or she) is never called upon to show what they can do.

There is, however, one fact that stands out and that is the knowledge that after the game or over, the crowds have left and the years go by, the team player – being the star or the man who stood on the side – will have inside him something far more important than athletic skill. He will have the ability to try, to continue to try, to never give up and to work and hope for the success of some larger endeavor than just for himself. Old heroes pass on and are forgotten but what is inside a person remains for the rest of his life and that spirit touches all those who are in constant contact with him.

Printed in the United States
By Bookmasters